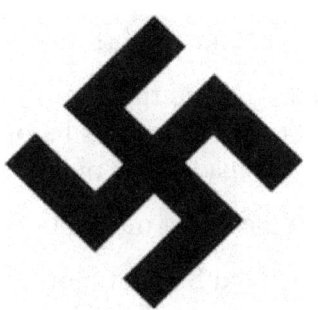

Art Sleuths,

An adventure/romance novel from the Great Depression to the Great War

by

Richard Everett Londgren

A KRONA PRESS BOOK
©2013

Foreword

Might (and money) makes right!

Napoleon learned long ago that loot of war becomes the fruit of war. So did lots of leaders before him and after him. Art of all kinds made easy pickin's.

Hitler looted with the worst of them.

In this story, the United States finally learned to go undercover to get evidence that might help convict Nazis involved in such brazen plunder.

Afraid that post-war conviction of Nazis for crimes against humanity might fail, the American secret service took a lesson from prosecution of crime at the time of the Great Depression. Can't convict criminals for bootlegging—get them for income tax evasion. Just in case.

So our Art Sleuths, operating out of Scandinavia, capitalized on American and Swedish neutrality as long as possible to gather evidence of Nazi art theft during World War II. Then they continued their covert operation—carefully—during the war itself.

But major crime by the Nazi leaders proved to be more than sufficient for their conviction. So legal concern about Nazi art theft became moot.

But for later art collectors, the provenance related to questionable ownership of art continued to raise concerns. So our Art Sleuths applied their knowledge and skills to investigate ongoing issues about possession of art.

In the process, they worked themselves into peacetime danger.

Contents

Chapter 1: A LOOK AHEAD, to LOS ANGELES, 2009

"Amazing! Wild! Even that doesn't begin to describe the bizarre scene here tonight.

"Well, I'm Rex Lyon, and welcome to our 'Lyon's Lair'. You folks in the studio audience should consider yourselves lucky to be here. You had to be chosen by lottery because so many wanted in. In fact, I was lucky to get through all the security myself.

"And what a circus we have outside, with those hoping to get in, others protesting with signs, and contending sides hollering at each other. They include cultural representatives from many countries, dowagers from museum boards, directors of galleries, even church archivists as well as individual collectors. Plus a bunch who are just curious.

"Well, let me remind folks in our TV audience that we do take on some controversial topics in the 'Lyon's Lair,' so occasional commotion may not be so unusual.

"But here's the strange part. The topic for tonight's show is art. How could that stir up so much excitement...and controversy?

"Judging by the reactions in the media earlier and by our hecklers outside, you'd think our topic might be da Vinci. Not so.

"You in the studio warmed up before the show by practicing our 'Lyons' Roar'. So let's hear you roar now as we bring in our controversial guest—if he was able to successfully run the gauntlet outside."

In contrast to the sustained roar from the audience in the "Lyon's Lair," the guest approached Rex Lyon briskly and calmly, tall and slim in his casual attire, with a hint of a puzzled look on his handsome face.

"Welcome, Karl Nelson," said Rex as he reached out to shake hands with the gray-haired guest.

"Glad to be here," laughed Karl. "Or at my age, glad to be anywhere."

When Rex and the audience finished laughing, Rex explained: "It isn't every day we have a nonagenarian, so we are especially thankful you weren't scared off."

"That's a pretty fancy word for an old geezer like me," said Karl. "Sounds pretty impressive, though."

"Well, time's a wastin'!" declared Rex, "so let's get right to the reason for all this hullabaloo about art. I gather that you're quite a successful artist, so have you painted your way into a corner of controversy?"

"You can judge for yourself," smiled Karl, as he pointed to his paintings and sculpture on display. "I call my work 'linear impressions,' and you can recognize my interest in architecture in the shapes and colors that prevail in varied ways."

"Your art commands a huge following...and huge prices, I might add," laughed Rex. "I think even da Vinci would admire your work...and income. But I don't see your art as the cause of a human hurricane."

"I consider my art to be pleasing to look at and stimulating to think about," explained Karl, as he waved to the left of his display. "But, as you no doubt realize, art is more than what meets the eye.

Some art is hot, some not—depending on how the critics react. Like the acclaim for Andy Warhol. Or, in my case, by the heat from all directions."

"So how do you explain the storm you seemed to have caused?"

"Well, for many years I've been what you might call an 'art sleuth,' and recently I've gone from the frying pan into the fire. Deliberation about ownership of art has heated up, as you probably know," explained Karl.

"Yup," said Rex, "the pressure is on for museums and other 'caretakers' of art to give back some of their collection to the original owners. Now they're just being called 'takers,' and the battle is on.

"What put you in the middle of all this, Karl?"

"By tracking art and other valuables lost by owners—including by countries as well as individuals—I've generated conflict and anger. But I'm not the jury, just the sleuth. Still, the results of my investigation often seem to generate a response of 'shoot the messenger' for bringing the report."

"I certainly can't call you paranoid," laughed Rex, "because they really are out to get you. Yet, you seem to be cool under fire, so to speak," said Rex. "Just how long have you had this investigative responsibility?"

"Since before World War II."

"Wow, you've been in that hot-seat for nearly 70 years!" exclaimed Rex, as many in the audience gasped.

"That deserves a rare repeat of our 'Lyon's Roar'!" shouted Rex, so the studio audience let loose with a blast that almost shook the rafters.

"That roar calls for more," said Rex, "and we'll be back after the break."

Chapter 2: A LOOK BACK TO LAKE SUPERIOR, THE YEAR 1937

Beggars can't be choosers, thought Karl Nelson, as he moved cautiously on the icy deck of the Lake Superior ship. *In the middle of the Depression, I'm lucky to get this job. Actually,* he corrected his thought, *I'm lucky Dad got me this job. Even his influence wouldn't help in the summer, when lots of men want this work. Most don't want to freeze their butts off this time of year. Well, besides making money for college, I get to learn a bit about what Dad has to deal with as a naval architect.*

"Well, college boy, what do you think of this breeze from Canada?" kidded First Mate Ivan Kaposki.

"A little rocky, isn't it, now that we don't have that load of iron ore to keep us steady. Hope you don't get sea sick!"

"I'm sick of this weather," responded Karl, with a grin to answer the ribbing.

"Duluth will look mighty good," said Ivan. "We'll have a couple days to load up and warm up."

"What's all that iron ore used for?" asked Karl, as they moved to protection from the wind.

"Not as much used as before, with the steel business down, as the auto assembly lines slowed down, not to mention the other factories cutting back on steel products," explained Ivan.

"I heard the Depression might get worse in '37, so I might have to go to work for old John D.," said Ivan.

"Who?" asked Karl.

"Rockefeller," said Ivan. "He ships oil in tankers, and that business still seems steady."

"Yeah, I heard that from my dad," said Karl, "because he's working on designs for Rockefeller's special piers in Duluth."

"Good man, your dad," said Ivan. "He's helped make these 'lakers' better…and safer. We lost some of these boats in the past because a load would shift in a storm. I've had a few close calls myself.

"You going to follow in his footsteps, now that you're getting some real experience?"

"Sort of," explained Karl, "except I want to stick to dry land. I hope to study architecture at the University of Wisconsin, and this 'real experience' will help pay my way."

"Good for you!" said Ivan, as he slapped Karl on the back. "I hope my kids at least finish high school. Maybe one of them will want to go to college."

"Hope so, too," said Karl. "Not easy in these tough times. I'll probably be washing dishes in the college cafeteria to survive."

"Some more 'real experience'," laughed Ivan. "But you should keep warm there…and safe!"

"Thanks, Dad, for getting me work in the port after the lake froze over and the boats quit running," said Karl, as he discussed his future with his dad, Bengt.

"With the ice breaking up, we'll have plenty of workers for the summer," said Bengt. "Now you should be getting ready for college. But your delay of a year seems like a good decision. Hope you've saved up some of your pay."

"Most of it," grinned Karl. "Couldn't spend much working on the boat, and the ports weren't interesting. But I learned a lot hearing about your work, and Mom provided lots of books about art. And lots of advice about my drawing."

"She thinks you have loads of talent. So do I!

"Planning to try out for the football team at Wisconsin? Your winter work should've got you ready."

"Naw, that's big-time stuff," said Karl. "If I'm lucky, I'll probably be serving food at the training table," laughed Karl.

"Speaking of getting ready, I thought I'd try to learn some more about architecture this summer, if I can. Uncle Bill has talked about that radical architect down his way. You know, Frank Lloyd Wright. Uncle Bill knows some of the workers at the place called Taliesin. I guess they come by for lumber and other building materials once in a while. A smart bunch, he said, and he thinks I might be able to get a job there. And learn a lot. Not much pay—maybe nothing but some meals—but Uncle Bill said I could camp out at their place."

"We'd miss you," said Bengt, "but you'd have a good time with our clan in Richland Center. You might get a running start in architecture if you can connect with Tally...what is it, again?"

"Taliesin," said Karl.

"I guess we're about ready to take a tour of Wisconsin, aren't we, Tina?" said Bengt, as he checked the load in the camper. "We'll celebrate Decoration Day with Bill and family. For a small town, Richland Center does it up big, with a parade and community activities. And I appreciate the many who visit the cemetery to honor those lost in wars."

"Should be fun driving the length of Wisconsin," said Tina. "I made some sandwiches, brought a batch of cookies and put juice in the cooler."

"Another rolling picnic," smiled Bengt, as he reflected about earlier jaunts. "We haven't done this for a while. Not much traveling in these tough times."

"Great to take another spin in our land yacht," said Karl, as he patted the side of the converted bus. "Lot more comfortable than that Great Lakes boat."

"Good work on welding the frames for the folding table and bunks, Karl. They're not coming apart at the seams," commented Bengt, as he looked over the interior.

"Helps to have an architectural engineer as teacher and inspector," laughed Karl. "I learned a lot assisting you as chief flunky. The scrap metal and pipes from the port sure fit the job for the rack we put on top."

"Still going strong—no leaks in the roof, either," added Bengt.

"Hey, Mom, our Viking ship design still looks great on the side of our yacht! Sure gets a lot of attention, sailing on those abstract waves you included in the design," admired Karl.

"For once, you had to color within the lines when you painted the design," smiled Tina. "Good discipline in contrast to the free style you favor."

"I'd say this 'yacht,' as you call it, has provided lots of learning opportunity—for all of us," reflected Bengt.

"Fun to work together, too!" said Tina.

"Even overhauling the engine made an interesting challenge," admitted Karl. "But I don't know if I'll ever get rid of the grease under my fingernails."

"Well, after all our self-praise, let's hit the road," said Bengt. "May be a long time before we can travel together again in our yacht. Good to have a back-up driver."

"Make that two," corrected Tina. "I can double-clutch with the best of you truck drivers!"

"Oops! Let my male mistake be a lesson to you, Karl.

"Well, I imagine you'll go directly to Madison at the end of summer. Got everything you need for college—including your acceptance and scholarship forms?"

"Yup, sure do."

"Think you'll have a chance to renew your friendship with Sonja?" wondered Tina.

"Maybe, but her head start at the university in Michigan put some distance between us," said Karl. "The letters are getting farther apart, too."

"Well, there are lots of fish in the sea," smiled Bengt. But when he saw Tina's frown, he added: "Not many with the superior qualities of Sonja, though. Or your mother."

"Good recovery, Dad," laughed Karl. "Another male lesson, I believe."

Chapter 3: RICHLAND CENTER, WISCONSIN, THE YEAR 1937

"What a treat, to come back to this beautiful area with its rolling hills and fields and forests," said Tina, as they approached Richland Center.

"Yeah, I always get a warm feeling about the area and this small town," echoed Bengt, "not to mention the comfortable hospitality of Bill and his family."

"That goes for me too," said Karl, "and I look forward to spending a longer time here."

When they rolled up to the craftsman house on the tree-lined street, Bill and Kirsten rushed out the door when they saw the camper approaching, with 12-year-old Eric and 10-year-old Ingrid right behind. Then the welcome included handshakes and hugs all around.

"You all look great," said Kirsten, "but you're probably weary after your long drive."

"No, we traveled in comfort," said Tina. "Karl even took a nap about half-way here."

"Your motor home sure looks cozy," said Bill. "Wouldn't mind taking a nap there too."

"When do we get a tour?" asked Eric.

"You'll have to wait, because I've got supper almost ready," said Kirsten. "We weren't sure when you'd arrive, so I just have to finish what I started."

As Bill surveyed Karl, he couldn't avoid blurting out a typical response about change in kids: "You sure have grown, Karl. And you sure look like you fit with that Viking ship painted on your vehicle!"

"How tall are you, Karl?" asked Eric.

"I'm finally as tall as Dad, at six-two," said Karl. "Hope I'm still growing, too."

"Me too!" responded Eric.

"Sailing must have been good for you, because you look as tough as nails," said Bill.

"I can hardly wait to show you off to my friends," said Ingrid. "I hope you like to swim."

"Sure do," said Karl, as he put his arm around Ingrid.

During supper, Bill thanked Bengt for coming. "Our lumber and hardware business is just eking along, so we're pinching pennies rather than traveling."

"We're careful, too," explained Bengt. "My job is not exactly what I'd hope for, but it's steady. Tina only teaches part-time, but she does enjoy the connection with art. Not surprising these days—both of us had our pay cut. Fortunately, Karl got work at the port so he could save up for college. Bringing him here over the holiday gave us a good reason to see you folks."

"Hope you plan to stay here this summer, Karl" said Bill. "We're counting on it."

"Yeah, we want to do lots of things with you," added Eric.

"Yeah, with me, too," echoed Ingrid.

"That's my plan," said Karl, "so I've counted on it too. Hope I can help with your lumber and hardware, Uncle Bill."

"My friend from Taliesin really perked up when he heard of your talents," said Bill. "So he looks forward to getting a helping hand from you.

Should be a great chance to learn—if not earn," smiled Bill.

"Many of the people there do lots of physical work around the place," explained Kirsten, "even though several already have degrees in architecture. Or are in college now."

"We have some cute girls at church," said Eric. "Some are home from college, so you should find them interesting. So are some of the high school boys, like Karla's brother, Andrew."

"I'll introduce you to my friend Karin at church," said Ingrid, "and she can introduce you to her older sister, Karla. She's really pretty."

"Karl and Karla—that would be a good combination," laughed Eric.

"Karla just finished her first year at the University," explained Kirsten, "so she might be a good advisor, Karl. And she's interested in art. Good athlete too. Especially skiing. Besides, she's a lot of fun."

"Guess I'll have to consider skiing," smiled Karl, "instead of spending winter on an ore boat."

"Well, the summer looks promising for you, Karl," said Tina, with a smile of satisfaction, and Bengt offered a slight smile, too.

Supper included wide-ranging reminiscing, plus nutritious food, mostly home-grown. Eric plied Karl with questions about sports, and was pleased to hear about Karl's success in football, basketball and track.

"I'm trying to learn to play tennis," said Ingrid, "and more about swimming."

"We didn't have tennis at my high school, so maybe you can teach me," said Karl.

"Well, I can't teach you much," answered Ingrid, "but I will take you along to meet our coach. You'll like her, too."

"Sounds as though your social calendar is filling already, thanks to Ingrid," said Kirsten, in her warm and reassuring voice.

"Speaking of your calendar," said Bill, "will you be available right after the holiday to meet Ted Jamison from Taliesin? He's coming for a load of lumber."

"Sure, and I'd be glad to help with the loading," said Karl.

"And, if you want to help him unload, that could be a good way for you to meet some of the 'students' at Taliesin," said Bill. "That would give you a chance to size up that interesting place and see how you might fit in."

"Great!" said Bengt. "Karl can get started in his new direction, while we're heading north again."

"Karl, sounds as though you got a good start on your independence by sailing on the Great Lakes," said Kirsten, "so you should enjoy another adventure and challenge here."

"We'll help," said Eric.

"And it seems that Ingrid has some interesting plans for Karl, too," said Bill, with his hand on Ingrid's shoulder.

Before his parents headed for home following their short visit, Karl got his initial introduction to the community during the coffee hour after the Sunday worship services at Our Savior's Lutheran Church.

But it proved to be a disappointment for Ingrid. "I guess the Lindholms are gone for the holiday, Karl, so you won't get to meet them."

"Maybe another time," said Karl, who felt a bit of disappointment too.

But soon all the Nelsons were enjoying the refreshments and fellowship in the friendly congregation.

"This sure gives me a good feeling about your community," Tina confided to Kirsten. "Karl has been a bit saddened recently because his girlfriend has faded out of his life, so this change should be good."

"We'll do our part to make his life here enjoyable for him," said Kirsten.

"Thanks," said Tina. "I can sense that already, with Eric and Ingrid leading the way."

On Tuesday morning, right after the holiday, the rickety Ford flatbed truck from Taliesin pulled into the Nelson lumberyard.

When the lanky middle-aged driver climbed out, he spotted Karl sorting lumber.

"You must be the nephew Bill told me about. No mistaking that. You definitely look related."

"That's me," said Karl. "I'm Karl Nelson, and guess we do look a lot alike."

"I'm Ted Jamison, and if you're like Bill in others ways, I say I'm very pleased to meet you. I heard that you're interested in architecture, so I told Bill that you might like to connect with the 'students' at Taliesin. Maybe even meet the Wrights."

"Are you one of the students?" asked Karl.

"I'm interested in learning," said Ted, "but not in a formal way like most of the others. I'm more of the flunky jack-of-all-trades who helps keep the place from falling apart. Well, that's an exaggeration, because the others pitch in with lots of the grunt work, too.

"I heard that you're not only an artist, but capable in lots of practical skills."

"My dad is an architectural engineer, and I learned a little of everything from him," said Karl. "I might even be able to help make your truck run better."

"Great! Someone who doesn't mind getting his hands dirty. And I hope you are a better mechanic than I am," said Ted.

"Hey, Ted!" came a shout from the entrance to the hardware store. "Looks like you're getting acquainted with my nephew."

"We're getting along swell," said Ted. "He's my kind of guy—just like you. Mind if I take him along to Taliesin today so he get a look at our circus?"

"I guess that makes all three of us counting on it," said Bill. "I told Karl that Taliesin could be a great place to learn about architecture."

"You might be shocked by some of the ideas, though," said Ted, "because the architecture at Taliesin isn't just copying the past."

"That suits me," said Karl, "because I like experimenting in art and in building."

"Can Karl get room and board there, or what kind of arrangement might be best?" asked Bill.

"I have a trailer house, and he can stay with me," said Ted. "We have plenty of plain food, mostly raised by us. We can stay flexible. If I or someone else from Taliesin isn't coming this way on the weekend, he can hitchhike. The traffic is steady on the highway, and most drivers are glad to give someone from Taliesin a ride. They consider it an interesting experience," laughed Ted.

"Okay by you, Karl?" asked Bill.

"Yup. It does sound like an interesting experience," laughed Karl.

"Okay," said Bill. "Let's load your lumber so you two can head for Taliesin."

"We won't load much," said Ted. "We're trying to pay as we go. But we do thank you, Bill, for the credit you've extended already."

Chapter 4: TALIESIN, THE YEAR 1937

At Taliesin, Ted drove the sputtering truck up toward a structure on a slope of the grounds.

"That's an interesting design," said Karl, as they approached a simple shed-roof building.

"Basically a storage building, but it does have distinctive beauty," said Ted. "You'll meet the designer later. She's one of the students here."

"Do you have mechanic's tools here?" asked Karl. "I meant it when I said I could work on your truck. At least check the plugs and carburetor."

"We have an assortment," said Ted. "After lunch, we can look 'em over."

During a lunch of fresh vegetables, berries, cheese, milk and homemade bread, Ted introduced Karl to those sitting nearby.

Naturally, Karl was asked if he is an architect.

"Nope," he said simply, "a sailor."

"What! A Viking sailor here on the prairie?" wondered another.

"Well, a short-time sailor on the Great Lakes," said Karl, "but I'll start at the University in the fall. In art and architecture. Hope what I can learn here will give me a head start."

"Don't count on it," laughed another 'student'. "Learning here might put you in a hole with the faculty at the University."

"Learn what you can here, but keep it quiet at the University," smiled a woman in the group.

"Karl was just admiring our storage building you designed," said Ted.

"That clinches it," she responded. "We now know that Karl is destined to go far in our trade!"

"You referred to a trade," said Karl. "Is that how you define architecture?"

"Don't take Nancy too literally," explained another. "But architecture does combine art and the building trades."

"Not a surprise to me, actually," said Karl. "My dad is a naval architect, which for him means mainly designing and refining the docks of Duluth and retrofitting the boats that haul ore and oil and grain on the Great Lakes."

"With this economy," said another, "he can consider himself lucky to be employed."

In the storage shed, Ted and Karl sorted and arranged the tools, so Karl could tune up the truck.

Then he cleaned the carburetor, filed and reset the spark plugs, checked the points and adjusted the distributor. After he started the truck, he grinned as he heard the smooth humming of the engine.

Smiling appreciatively, Ted shook hands with Karl, and then they laughed about their greasy hands.

Art Sleuths

When a growing cluster of students at supper heard about the truck, one student called for help repairing the tractor. "It misfires half the time and can hardly pull its own weight." He begged jokingly, "We need your help. Or at least our tractor does."

"Anyone willing to lend a hand?" asked Karl. "As Ted knows, it could be messy. And maybe frustrating, depending on whether we can repair the tractor or not."

"Call me Hank, and count me in," said a student. "I've dealt with some of that kind of mess and frustration before," he added. "Besides, it should beat weeding the garden and digging rocks."

Later, when the tractor just coughed occasionally rather than all the time, Karl gained acceptance among the students, and occasionally joined in—or at least listened in on—their discussions and deliberations about architectural projects in the works or under consideration.

When they heard about Karl's drafting skills, several asked for a showing. After Karl brought out some samples, his fellow "students" complimented him on his appealing depictions of buildings—with watercolors over India ink.

With that kind of support and encouragement, Karl soaked up ideas about materials, the engineering related to structures, and the pragmatics of systems such as heating and ventilating.

From his art studies in high school and the tutoring by his mother, he offered useful opinions about color selection and application.

Toward the end of Karl's second week, Ted suggested that he could take a few days off. "I'm heading to Richland Center again, so come along, and then come back when you're refreshed."

"Sounds good to me," said Karl. "Besides, I want to check on some art supplies anyway."

When they arrived in Richland Center Friday afternoon, Ted stopped on Main Street. "Here's a stationery store that carries some art supplies. Enjoy yourself there, and I'll tell Bill that you'll see them at supper. And I'll see you Monday—or whenever."

As he hopped out of the truck, Karl reached back inside to shake hands. "Thanks a lot, Ted. I'm learning a lot, and enjoying it too."

"You sure fit in," said Ted, "and already contribute in several ways. See you next week."

As Karl entered the small stationery shop, called THE BREV, an attractive young blonde behind the counter looked up and started to say, "What can I do…?"

After pausing, she said with a smile, "I'm Karla, and I think I'm supposed to meet you."

"I think that's my line. I'm Karl, and I think I'm supposed to meet you," laughed Karl.

Karla reached out to shake hands, and then explained: "Your cousin Ingrid and my sister Karin have been conspiring to be matchmakers. So far they've been frustrated. Won't this surprise them!"

"How did you know who I am?" asked Karl.

"Your hat," laughed Karla. "The name Nelson reversed in the shape of a saw. I have a special liking for that, because I designed it for your uncle."

"When I first put it on, I liked that simple but strong design," said Karl, with a slight smile. "Now I definitely think it's a **great** design."

"I heard that you're interested in art," said Karla, "including the art of flattery. But thanks for the compliment."

"I plan to study art, art history and architecture at the University," said Karl. "I was told that you might give me some pointers about the University and the courses."

"Sure. But I'll trade you," said Karla. "You can tell me about Taliesin."

"Well, I need to get back to Taliesin Monday, so can we get together soon? Say, tomorrow night?" asked Karl.

"Oh, a man of action, for sure," laughed Karla. "Well, my boyfriend's in Madison, so I'm free—at least for some conversation about art."

"Our store doesn't close until 9 tomorrow night," said Karla. "Maybe we could chat while you walk me home, and then you could meet that little matchmaker Karin and the rest of my family.

"By the way, as I started to ask, what can I do for you?"

"I had planned to look over your art supplies...but I got distracted. I'll check later...give me a reason to come back," said Karl. "Now I'd better report to Ingrid, my little matchmaker."

The other Nelsons were eager to hear the report about Karl's first two weeks, so the usual wholesome supper was spiced up with his descriptions of the people, the buildings and the activities at Taliesin.

"Just like you indicated, Uncle Bill, Taliesin doesn't claim to be an ordinary school...or business. It's more like an ongoing dialogue about architecture, with some necessary work thrown in for survival."

"Ted Jamison already gave you high marks, Karl, for your willingness to help and for your considerable skills," said Bill. "He was most impressed that you got their old tractor functioning, and he said the other students there already appreciate your skills related to architecture."

"I've sure met some interesting people," said Karl, "and I've already learned a lot more about architecture."

"Well," asked Kirsten, "have you met Mr. Wright yet?"

"Nope, I guess he was away all that time," said Karl. "He's had a bunch of commissions recently, including some in Wisconsin. A big one in Racine. I do hope to meet him some time.

"But I did meet another interesting person a short time ago," added Karl. "I believe her name is Karla."

"You met Karin's sister, Karla?" exclaimed Ingrid.

"You did?" exclaimed a surprised Kirsten.

"By accident," said Karl. "I went in the stationery store to look for art supplies. And there she was, behind the counter. And just as pretty as you said, Ingrid."

"Did you ask her out?" asked Ingrid, as the others smiled and waited for the answer.

"Oh yes, but she has a boyfriend in Madison," said Karl.

"Too bad," said a dejected Ingrid.

"But I am going to walk her home tomorrow night after her store closes," said Karl, as Ingrid let out a whoop.

"She acknowledged that we could at least talk about art, even though she has a boyfriend. And she's curious about Taliesin," said Karl.

"Pretty smooth," said Eric.

"By the way, I learned that she designed the graphics for your business, Uncle Bill," added Karl, with a slight smile. "And even before I knew that, I liked the design. Of course, now I think it's truly great art!"

At 8:45 Saturday evening, Karl dropped in at THE BREV. The name reminded him he needed to write home, as he looked at the art supplies while he waited for Karla to get off work. She introduced him to her boss, George Lundstrom, owner of the store.

"I understand you're helping out at Taliesin," said George. "You should learn a lot, and you'll find all of the people there to be interesting and highly creative. They come in here occasionally, even Mr. Wright. I, personally, am honored to be associated with them."

As Karl and Karla strolled the six blocks to her home, she plied him with questions about Taliesin and he asked about her study at the University.

"I have to admit," said Karl, as they approached her house, "that Ingrid was greatly disappointed to learn that you have a boyfriend. So am I, actually. But Ingrid was relieved that he is far away in Madison. And so am I, actually."

Karla laughed, and said: "As I mentioned before, you're certainly skilled in the art of flattery."

"But will it get me somewhere?" asked Karl.

"Well, it will get you into our house to meet the rest of my family," she said with a smile, as she opened the door.

Inside, Karin rushed up to them. "I'm so glad you got to meet. Ingrid and I were planning it."

"I heard that you two matchmakers were plotting," laughed Karl.

"Karl, meet my mom and dad, Henrik and Elin, and my brother, Andrew."

After they all shook hands, including Karin, Elin announced that cake and hot chocolate were ready, "if you're interested."

"Count me in," said Karl, as Karin directed him to the dining room.

"Great house!" said Karl, as he admired the beams and wood paneling.

"Not exactly a Taliesin design," said Henrik, "but we like this Craftsman style."

"Yeah, I've read about the Greene brothers, and their many Craftsman houses. Good to have a chance to see one of that style," said Karl.

"I can show you the rest of it another time," said Karla, "with all its unusual features."

"Maybe I can see some of your art, too," said Karl.

"Are you an artist, like Karla?" asked Elin.

"I kinda mix art and architecture," said Karl. "My dad is a naval architect and my mother teaches art in our high school. I suppose that explains my combination."

"We display art at the store," said Karla. "Maybe we could show yours. Do you have any here?"

"Well, I do have a portfolio to present as part of my enrollment at the University," said Karl. "I'd be interested in your opinion."

"You look more like an athlete than an artist," said Andrew, "but I guess I don't really know what an artist might look like."

"Like Karla," said Karl, with a smile.

"I'm sort of both," continued Karl. "I played lots of high school sports. And I've painted about sports, too."

Gradually, Karl learned more about the Lindholm family—Henrik a doctor and Elin a nurse. And he learned more about their community and their Lutheran church.

"We're going to 11:00 church tomorrow morning," said Karin. "We have coffee, juice and snacks afterward. Can you come? I want to show you off to my friends."

"Mine too," said Andrew, with a grin.

"Well, then, mine too," said Karla, with a laugh.

After Karl left, Henrik smiled and declared: "Karla, you've really found a match in Karl. And I don't mean just in name. He's extraordinary."

"Wait—I didn't find him," laughed Karla. "He just wandered into our store."

"Well, Ingrid and I would have got the two of you together if we'd had a chance," protested Karin.

"He seems like a great guy, so hang onto him, I'd say," added Andrew.

"In contrast," commented Elin, "after half a year, we haven't even met your boyfriend from Madison."

"I'll bet we would get to meet him soon enough if we alerted him about Karl," said Andrew, with a wicked grin.

As Karla lay thinking before falling asleep that night, she smiled to herself about this strange situation with her, her family and Karl.

Here I am, she thought, *almost committed to an outstanding literature major at the University, a recognized poet and the son of a professor. And now this sailor who wants to be an artist stumbles into my life. And I'm attracted to him. Well, tomorrow*

*morning might be an interesting test of responses
from others.*

At the Nelsons', Karl stretched out in bed. *This
feels great, after the makeshift bed at Taliesin,* he
thought. *I can hardly believe all my interesting
experiences after just a couple of weeks. And what a
strange coincidence, going into the store where
Karla works. Hope I can enjoy her friendship and
learn from her without getting too attached. But she
sure helps me forget Sonja!*

In the Nelson church pew, Ingrid jabbed Karl
in the side. "There she is," she whispered, as she
discretely indicated the Lindholms' pew ahead of
them at the right.

"Shouldn't you be in Sunday School,"
whispered Karl, "instead of matchmaking?"

"No Sunday School in the summer," answered
Ingrid, with a snicker.

"She sings well, too," grinned Ingrid, as
Kirsten shushed her.

The worship service was reassuring to Karl
with its familiar liturgy and music, and the pastor's
sermon about salvation through belief in Christ
caused him to try to visualize what heaven might
look like.

After the service, the Nelsons formed a
phalanx led by Ingrid, heading for the fellowship
room. Bill got coffee for Kirsten and Karl, while
Eric brought a sweet roll for Karl and another for
himself. "Take it from an expert, these are the best,"
he announced.

Soon the Lindholms caught up with them, and
Henrik mentioned to Bill and Kirsten how much
they enjoyed meeting Karl.

Art Sleuths

While Eric and Ingrid were rounding up their friends to meet Karl, Karla touched his arm. "Oops! Hope I didn't cause you to spill your coffee," she apologized, "but I want you to meet some of my friends."

Holding his arm lightly, she led him to a cluster of young men and women, who greeted Karla and Karl with a smile and a mixture of "good morning, hello, glad you could be here." As Karla introduced them, he tried to connect a face and features with a name.

Anja in particular caught his eye, as he noted her auburn hair, pretty face and shapely figure.

"Watch out, you girls," said Karla, "because Karl is a sailor new in town, and he has a keen eye for beauty."

"I can see that," said Jim, with a laugh, as he glanced at Karla.

"Are you really a sailor?" asked Tom.

"Was…and it was only on Lake Superior in a boat hauling iron ore," explained Karl.

"Now he's working at Taliesin," said Karla.

"I think that's more threatening than being a sailor," laughed Susan. "That commune includes a strange bunch, from what I've seen when they come to town."

"Guess that makes me strange then, so watch out," laughed Karl. "But maybe some day you'd like to visit there."

"Let's!" said Anja. "I've heard so much about their creative designs. Maybe that would inspire me."

At that moment, Ingrid and Karin came to drag Karl away. "The younger kids want to meet Karl, too," said Ingrid.

With a refill of coffee and another sweet roll, Karl asked them about their interests. "Eric, what do you hope to be?"

"Well, like my dad, I like to work with wood, so maybe I'll build houses," answered Eric. "If you'll design them, Karl."

"It's a deal," said Karl, as he sought responses from others.

"I want to be a writer," said Ingrid. "Then maybe I could write about your life as a sailor. That sounds exciting."

"Well, it sure was when a storm hit Lake Superior," said Karl.

That caused other kids to ask about the dangers of sailing, and the Nelsons and Lindholms and a few other adults listened to the dramatic stories Karl told about life on a laker, plying the Great Lakes.

Karla and Anja joined the circle of listeners, and Karla whispered to Anja, "Beware, he's a flirt as well as a storyteller."

"Intriguing," smiled Anja.

As the families were leaving the church, Bill suggested to Karl that he escort Karla home. "Anja lives near her, so you could accompany both of the girls."

So Karl announced to Karla and Anja: "I've been assigned to escort both you home. Security on an early Sunday afternoon," he laughed, as they laughed at the risk.

"So gallant!" exaggerated Karla, as Anja smiled in response.

After a few blocks, Anja announced, "Here's my place. I'll catch up with you later, Karla. Great talking with you, Karl. Hope to see you soon. Swimming in the park, perhaps."

"Yeah, Eric has already invited me," said Karl. "Maybe we can all meet there. I'll let Eric decide when."

At her door, Karla touched Karl's arm and thanked him for being so thoughtful to the kids. "They sure were enchanted by your stories. Well, so was I," she added.

"When will you be back?" she asked.

"Probably the end of the week, but you never know with that unpredictable crew," he explained.

"I'd sure like to see your paintings," said Karla. "Maybe you could bring them to the store, so George could see them, too. He's a great judge of art."

"Thanks. I look forward to the response from you and George—I think. Anyway, I'll come by as soon as I can. And I want to see your art—as soon as I can.

"Already, you seem like a long-time friend," he added. "I'll miss you."

"Hurry back," she said softly, as she put her hand on his arm.

Two weeks later, he hitchhiked 'home' on Friday afternoon. He caught a ride with a middle-aged husband and wife, and they were so absorbed in his stories about his life at Taliesin that they took him right to the Nelsons' house. They watched in appreciation as Ingrid, Eric and Kristen welcomed him with hugs. Then Karla and Anja came out the door. And, in the spirit of the moment, they both hugged him, too.

"Let me introduce you to my driver," laughed Karl, as he introduced them to Jim Karlstad. "And his able co-pilot, Barbara. We've had a great chat. They're graduates of the University, so I learned more about what to expect there.

"By the way, Karla is a student there now," added Karl.

"We've enjoyed our visit with you, Karl, and now meeting your family and friends," said Barbara, "Time for us to be on our way."

"Maybe we'll look for you folks again when we drive through Richland Center," said Jim, "because you and your town have made a great impression."

As the rest of them went in the house, Karla explained that "I thought you might be back to celebrate Independence Day with us, so I came over to welcome you. Anja felt the same way."

"You know what I'd like to do," said Kirsten, "let's all of our families get together for a picnic at the park late in the afternoon on the Fourth. You guys can swim earlier, and we can stay to watch the fireworks later."

"Great idea," said Karla.

"I think my family would love it, too," said Anja.

"Okay, alert your parents, to make sure they agree," said Kirsten. "Then I'll coordinate with them."

"Now," said Karla, "another reason I came by is to remind you, Karl, to bring your portfolio to the store tomorrow. George will be there in the morning, so could you come about 10?"

"I do believe I could make that, unless I have to work for Uncle Bill or around the house here," said Karl.

"Take up that offer for tomorrow morning," said Kirsten. "I want to hear what the two art experts have to say, also."

"So do I," said Anja.

"Well, come on down and put your two-cents' worth in, Anja," said Karla. "Hope you won't be overwhelmed, Karl?"

"I'll be delighted to have such an esteemed jury," said Karl.

As Karl opened his portfolio on a table in THE BREV, he explained: "I just prepared this drawing in connection with a project at Taliesin."

"Wow!" said George, "you are a superb draftsman, and the colors you've washed over the ink help create a wonderful effect. We'll be proud to display it here, if that's okay."

"You bet!" said Karl.

"I like this abstract design," said Karla. "Does it represent something?"

"Those are segments of steam pipes in the boat's boiler, and the misty colors are from the warning labels on and near the pipes," explained Karl. "And this is the moving of the pistons of the steam engine."

"Oh, I like this!" exclaimed Karla. "What is it?"

"These blues and greens and whites depict the water churned up by the boat's propeller," explained Karl.

"Another mystery," said Anja, as they looked at a circular pattern divided by bold shadows.

"Looking down at an open-pit iron mine," said Karl.

He moved on to a painting with dramatic splashes of red, brown, orange and shades of green.

"These colors seem different from what I've seen before," said George.

"Well, you might say they are unique," explained Karl, "because I made them in a special way. See those shades of red—I made the paints from oxidized iron ore. Well, I discovered patches of ore in the hold of the ship and worked them into thick paint."

"How about the yellows and oranges and greens?" asked George.

"I thank the Ojibways for that. I learned how they used plants and berries to create dyes, so I tried that too. And I used those colors to paint this portrait of an Ojibway friend. It seemed like a fitting acknowledgement.

"Here's another experiment with the thin dyes and thick ore paint," explained Karl as he showed a geometric design with varying colors and textures.

"Interesting," said George, "and powerful. How did you paint that?"

"I mixed scrapings from an empty cement bag with the dyes, then painted sections. When that dried, I taped strips from the paper cement bag over the dried colors to make patterns for other geometric shapes.

"Now here's the best part! I stood back and threw the iron colors in other masked areas. Sort of like throwing a football," he said with a grin as he demonstrated his throwing form.

"I told Andrew that I sometimes use sports as a theme. So here's my view focused on the back of a ball carrier, with the foreground and background muted in shape and color."

"Do you have more?" asked the surprised Karla.

"Well, I included just one illustration of a dock and storage building in Duluth as an example of a semi-realistic painting. I left most of those at home, but a couple of them have appeared in a shipping magazine."

"Even that seems like an impression," said George, "and I like the lines that emerge and fade and cross. Fits your interest in architecture.

"So I think we have the potential for an extraordinary exhibit, with you offering commentary," continued George. "If it's okay with you, I'll arrange a selection, create the labels and plan publicity. Maybe you could ask at Taliesin for permission to display your architectural drawing. That would have good publicity value as well as adding to the interesting contrasts of your art.

"Could you and Bill make frames that are dark and simple so they don't conflict with the art?" asked George. "I'm sure the Chamber of Commerce will reimburse Bill. Just cut and nail laths and stain them dark brown. You can't nail your thin painted panels to the frames, so just put a row of brads inside the back of the frames and secure the paintings to the brads with masking tape."

"We can handle that," said Karl. "Sounds simple. Fits my style—like cutting my 'canvas' from damaged Masonite panels I scrounged at the port."

"Good for you, Karl," commented George. "I like your improvising—and your economizing.

"In that spirit," said George, "could you make simple tripods out of laths to display your paintings? Just fasten the three legs at the top, and then attach a cross-piece from a lath about three feet up on the two front legs for a painting to rest on. A short length of twine to tie the cross-piece to the back leg should secure the angle."

"I'll help," said Karla. "Sounds like an interesting project."

"Me too," said Anja. "Should be good experience in case I ever have a chance to display my art."

"Well, this is really something," said Karl. "Thanks to all of you for your interest and help," said Karl, in a deep and soft voice, as he shook hands with George.

Then Karla hugged him, whispering: "I'm so proud of you!"

"Thanks for letting me be part of this," said Anja, as she too hugged him.

At the Fourth of July picnic, Karl met Anja's parents, Lars and Lena Andresson, and her younger brother, Arne.

"We're glad to meet the person who has inspired Anja to focus on her art again," said Lars.

"From what she's described, we're looking forward to an exhibit of *your* art," said Lena. "And hear about the goings-on at Taliesin."

"Anja said you painted a scene of a football player," said Arne. "I want to see that."

"Are you interested in art, too?" asked Karl.

"Actually, I'm more interested in football," admitted Arne, with a grin.

Then Ingrid and Karin approached with Anja in tow.

"I guess you already know my tennis coach," said Ingrid. "Maybe she'll let you take lessons, too."

"Anja—so that's why you have such a dark tan so early in the summer," said Karl, as he admired her tawny skin, set off by her yellow swimsuit.

"You seem to have a good tan, yourself," said Anja.

"Mine came from grueling labor in blistering heat, not just playing around in the sun," laughed Karl.

"Okay, let's set a date so you can work up a sweat playing in the sun," countered Anja.

"Did you hear that, Karin?" said Ingrid, "they're going on a date."

"I don't think so," said Karin. "Here comes her boyfriend now."

"Hi Dan, we were just talking about you," said Karin. "We thought you'd like to meet Karl Nelson. Ingrid's cousin."

"I feel like I know you already from what I've heard. I'm Dan Swanson," he said as he reached out to shake hands.

"I guess you've heard, I'm Karl Nelson. And I hope what you heard about me is all good."

"Karl's a friend of Anja," said Karin, "but Dan's a *real good* friend of Anja."

Then Arne joined in and announced: "I think it is time for them to arm-wrestle to see who's the best friend!"

"Oh, I can't," said Karl, "I might injure my painting arm."

"Anja did say that you're quite a painter," said Dan. "I look forward to the display of your art."

"Yeah, right now I'm painting some buildings at Taliesin," laughed Karl.

Others joined in the conversation, and Andrew pointed out that Karl paints football players, too.

"You should paint Dan," added Andrew. "He's a star at Augustana College, down in Illinois."

"You play, too?" asked Dan.

"In high school," said Karl, "but I'd get trampled on if I turned out at the University."

"So would I," laughed Dan.

"Anja is a cheerleader at Dan's school," said Ingrid, with pride in her voice.

"Well, I do find cheerleaders appealing, but my cheerleader just dumped me," said Karl.

"Oh, you poor boy!" said Karla.

"Hey, I know," said Anja, "you should arm-wrestle Karla's boyfriend to see who's the best friend!"

"Good idea, and my arm is feeling much stronger already," laughed Karl, and the others laughed with him.

During the fireworks, as Bill and Kirsten sat holding hands in the dark, she whispered, "This sure has been fun, and Karl adds so much to our family and friends. I miss him more every time he leaves."

"I feel the same way, and I'm so proud of him," said Bill.

"I'm sure looking forward to the display of his art," said Kirsten. "I haven't asked him to show us his paintings, because I want to wait to see them when George sets up the exhibit and Karl tells about the paintings."

Chapter 5: ART EXHIBIT, THE YEAR 1937

In a discussion back at Taliesin, Karl mentioned that a coming art show by a stationery

store in Richland Center would include his paintings.
"I've even been requested to be there to tell about
my art."

After the clapping, the others wanted to know
more.

"The simplest way would be for some of you
to drop by, because I've included a drawing I
prepared here. First, I want to know if my drawing
connected to Taliesin would be okay to show."

"It's your drawing, isn't it?" asked one.

"Yup!" said Karl.

"Then why not," said a student leader, and
others expressed agreement.

"If there's interest in connection with that
drawing, I thought I would tell about the creative
spirit of Taliesin," said Karl.

"Don't forget to tell about the grunt work,
too," came one response, accompanied by laughter.

"Keep us posted about the date, and we'll send
out our truth squad," said the leader, "to make sure
we're described in a positive way. That can be a
challenge sometimes."

At the evening meal, Karl raised another issue.
"At home, my dad the architect and my mother the
art teacher have talked about the influence of the
Bauhaus in Germany. Is that discussed here, because
your approach seems similar?"

"Let's say quietly that many of us agree with
the Bauhaus approach," said the same leader from
the earlier discussion, "but it could touch a nerve
with Mr. Wright."

"Why's that?" asked Karl.

"Don't broadcast this," came one response,
"but I think it is envy, because those German leaders

who fled Hitler and came here get so much attention."

"On the good side," said another, "I think it has caused us to respond in fresh ways to some of their design ideas."

"Okay, my lips are sealed," laughed Karl. "So let me switch to a different topic. I'm going to borrow my uncle's equipment to weld some broken parts on our mower.

"In appreciation for Uncle Bill's loan, I plan to make a 'perpetual motion' device to decorate his hardware store. I'll put a wick in a pipe that balances like a teeter-totter. One end will be down until the wicking of water shifts the weight to tip the other end down. Then the wick will reverse the action.

"My attempt at simple sculpture…and perpetual motion," smiled Karl. "Except in winter," he laughed.

"Should be intriguing," said another.

"Anyway, if you want some welding on a project, let me know, and I'll see if I can help," concluded Karl. "But keep in mind, my skills are limited."

"Sorry to embarrass you by parking the truck in front of your store," said Karl, as he greeted Karla and George. "Ted lent me the truck so I could bring some supplies back, including welding equipment on loan from Uncle Bill."

"That's okay," said George, "because a Taliesin truck gets the attention of shoppers."

"And do we ever have news for you, Mr. Rembrandt," said Karla with a wide smile. "Your exhibit will be the last weekend of the month, so we will have ample time to publicize it."

"Besides," said George, "we're borrowing a bigger space at the City Hall. The Chamber of Commerce sees it as good for business, so they will help promote the show and provide refreshments.

"One thing I wonder is whether you want to sell your paintings," said George.

"Well, I could use the money for college, so I guess the answer is 'yes'," answered Karl. "This is kinda new to me, though the shipping firm paid me to paint for them. Even if any painting sells, I might need to keep it long enough to show as part of my acceptance at the University"

"All right," said George, "but I'll try to establish a good valuation and promote selling, too."

"Be sure to plan for your commission," said Karl.

"We hadn't expected that," said George.

"But you've earned it," responded Karl. "I hope my paintings are worth enough so you make some money, too.

"Karla, I feel like celebrating with a malt next door," said a gleeful Karl. "Can you get time off to celebrate?"

"Sure she can," said George, "and the treat's on me!" he added, as he handed Karl some money.

"Thanks, George, for everything," said Karl as he shook hands with George.

Then he reached for Karla's hand, as they left to celebrate next door.

"Oops!" said Karl, as he released her hand. "I got carried away and encroached on your boyfriend's territory. Cost me a five-yard penalty, I imagine."

"That would spoil the celebration," she countered, with a smile, as she reached for his hand.

Art Sleuths

After supper, Karl took time to write home.

Hi Mom and Dad,

After my earlier letters with their routine news, this one will have some interesting news. At the end of the month, my paintings will be featured in a show at our City Hall, thanks to the help of the stationery store in town. This all started when I dropped in to check on art supplies. That led to an interest in the portfolio I had prepared to use as part of my admission at the University.

Anyway, the owner liked what he saw, and started the ball rolling. Now he's promoting the event and has even arranged to have my art for sale.

I hope some of the 'students' from Taliesin will take in the exhibit, because one piece is an architectural rendering I drew there and added splashes of watercolor for enhancement.

I am expected to be on hand to talk and answer questions, and I hope some of the Taliesin students will offer comments, because that would add considerable interest.

Sonja is fading from my thoughts, because Ingrid arranged for me to meet some attractive college girls at church. Unfortunately, they both have boyfriends, but they are fun to get to know anyway.

I've arranged to borrow Uncle Bill's welding equipment so I can create an eye-catching fountain for the front of his store. He is letting me take the equipment to Taliesin too, so I can weld some broken equipment there. I hope I haven't forgotten all you taught me about welding, Dad.

Taliesin continues to be very interesting, and I'm learning a lot from this creative group. I may not ever have a chance to meet Mr. Wright, because he's been away on a series of projects, including one in Racine. Another in Pennsylvania, called "Fallingwater," is getting a lot of favorable comment.

Hope all goes well with the two of you.
With love from Karl

Thanks to a barrage of publicity by George and the Chamber of Commerce, interest in the exhibit grew steadily. Karl's association with Taliesin got the attention from varied media. And the art and architecture departments at the University of Wisconsin indicated their desire to attend—and learn more about a future student.

"This may seem like a contradiction in communication," said George when he addressed a meeting of the C of C, "but a radio station in Madison wants to broadcast our art show."

At that, the C of C audience laughed and clapped.

"Maybe the Taliesin connection caught their attention," explained George, "but Karl Nelson's paintings connected to his work on a Great Lakes boat probably intrigue them, too. And the paint and paintings related to the Ojibways add another dimension.

"Whatever," continued George, "I appreciate the radio station for promoting the event, and I'll be intrigued with how they report about an art show. Well, I always thought that radio is a visual medium, so radio descriptions of Karl's art could create some memorable images in the minds of the listeners. Maybe enough to motivate them to come to Richland Center and see for themselves."

As the members of the C of C drifted away, they thanked George for creating this show and creating interest in the community.

"I think we have made a worthy investment in helping you with this event," said Charlie Williams, president of the C of C. "Personally, I think this will be extremely interesting, and I look forward to seeing... and hearing...the exhibit. I don't even want a preview. I just want to savor it fresh."

On the Saturday morning before the show, George and Karla walked Karl through the exhibit. "The printed descriptions are based on what we heard from you," said George, "so I hope we captured the essence of your thoughts."

"You sure did," said Karl, "because Karla showed me a draft...and it sounded great. She showed me the printed program, too, so I have a pretty good grasp of the situation."

"Thanks, Karla, for your good advance work," said George.

"As it turns out, the show will be broadcast by a Madison radio station," explained George. "Can you beat that! Broadcasting an art show!

"That means you'll have to explain and interpret your paintings, but in a casual and friendly way, just as you did in talking with us about your art," said George.

"Karla has arranged for Anja and Dan to be ready with some questions during any lulls in the event. Anja will ask about the painting of the pipes on the boat, and that will prime you to tell about your work on the Great Lakes and your dad's work as a naval architect."

"I'll be ready to ask you about your development of pigments from oxidizing iron ore," said Karla, as she touched Karl's hand. "That could give you a chance to talk about colors and the art training provided by your mother. And you could move on to the colors based on dyes used by the Ojibways. Then on to the portrait of your Ojibway friend."

"If there's time and need," said George, "Dan will ask about the football scene and your interest in sports. That could be an opening to talk about your semi-realistic paintings.

"Of course, we don't know what questions to expect from the audience," added George. "You met Charlie Williams of the Chamber of Commerce, and he may have some comments and questions.

"And here's something special. Representatives from the arts at the University of Wisconsin expect to be here to learn more about you and your work. If they like what they see and hear, you could get a great jump start at the University."

"As we had hoped," said Karl, "some of the Taliesin folks might drop by, so that could prove to be interesting—but probably unpredictable."

"That would be super!" said George. "I can't think of anything but good coming from that.

"Now, why don't the two of you relax and bolster each other for the show."

"Well, it's picnic time again, just like the Fourth," said Karla, "because I have a basket of food for us to share, and Anja and Dan will be here shortly."

"And the fireworks come next," laughed Karl.

"I guess we'd better open the doors a little ahead of time," George said to Charlie. "There's a long line of folks waiting. We should remind them that the exhibit will also be open after the interview with Karl and will stay open the rest of the week.

"Got your team ready to give directions and hand out programs?"

"You bet," said Charlie, "and this is looking good. I even saw about a dozen from Taliesin coming to town, sitting on the back of their flatbed truck."

"You guys really made that fun and funny!" exclaimed Charlie after the presentation by Karl and George. "Darn it! I might want to buy one of your paintings, Karl, even if I can't afford it."

"See my agent," laughed Karl, as he shook hands with Charlie and thanked him again.

"Oh, oh! Here comes trouble," smiled Karl, as a few Taliesin students approached.

He introduced them to George, as they complimented Karl about his unique and creative expressions.

"By the way," said Ted, "we drove by Bill's store and saw your fountain in action."

"Simple, but fascinating," said another.

Suddenly, the radio announcer reached with his microphone into the group, and he quickly got a variety of reactions. And he followed up with questions for the Taliesin students.

"Well," George asked the announcer, "what do you think about broadcasting an art show?"

"We gambled with the idea—and we won! Many of the explanations spoke for themselves in describing the art, so I didn't have to add much more. Even getting this big of a crowd for an art show in a small town is remarkable, so talking about that added another angle to our broadcast."

Later, two representatives of the University approached Karl. "We looked over your enrollment application before we came, and we were impressed by that," explained one, "and this show proved how advanced you are...and working with the folks at Taliesin must add significantly to your growth."

"I thank them, and for the years of influence and teaching by my dad and mother," said Karl.

"Yes, your application revealed their credentials," said the other University representative.

"Anyway, when you complete your enrollment, we're sure we can arrange an accelerated program, perhaps a scholarship...and a part-time position in our communication office."

When Karla came over to congratulate Karl, he introduced her to the University representatives.

"Yes, we're aware of you, too," said one. "We checked to see if we have students from here, and your name came up. Besides, we remember you from your classes. So it's good to see you again."

"Glad to know that you're lending a hand with a future student," said the other.

"It has been interesting...actually, quite exciting!" said Karla, as she glanced at Karl.

Karl suffered a letdown for a few days after his art show, despite the continuing publicity about his art. But then he got back in action at Taliesin, where he was asked to help with a variety of drawings. In turn, he got advice about the handling of perspective, and he continued to learn about the many practical aspects of architecture.

Others called on his welding skill to help with their metal sculpture.

Finally, after nearly two more weeks of his expanded and stimulating work at Taliesin, he announced that he would have to leave for the University.

The lunch gathering on Friday seemed subdued. Then the singing began by a few students: "For Karl's a grand guy, which nobody can deny, we'll miss his cheery face, when he leaves this place." For the refrain, they all sang it with gusto as Karl was beckoned to the front table.

Then a cheer went up, as Mr. Wright entered and walked over to shake hands with Karl. "So you're the young artist I've heard so much about.

"I'm told that your depiction of architectural details is outstanding, so I arranged to have one of my early drawings framed for you."

Karl stammered, and he finally spoke: "I'm so glad to meet you, and I thank you for this precious gift. I thank Taliesin for the opportunity to learn from the talented and creative…and helpful people here."

After the applause, several gathered around to ask him about his plans at the University, and to encourage him to come back soon. "We might need some more welding," laughed one, who slapped him on the back.

After lunch, he put his prized drawing by Mr. Wright in the cab of the truck, and several continued to chat with him while they helped load the welder on the flatbed. With the bundle of his few personal items, he climbed into the truck with Ted. He waved out the window as they headed toward Richland Center.

In town, Bill came out to meet them when they pulled up at the hardware store. With great pride, Karl showed the drawing, signed by Mr. Wright, with thanks to Karl. Other names from Taliesin filled the back.

"Can you guys unload the welder and my stuff?" asked Karl. "I have to show this to Karla…and George."

When they assured him they could, he shook hands with Ted and thanked him for his help and friendship.

"We'll miss you, Karl," said Ted. "My place will seem empty without you. So hurry back."

Karl dashed down the street and into the stationery store, where a startled and elated Karla looked up…exclaimed with joy and hurried around the counter to hug Karl. "I missed you so much!"

"Me too!" said Karl, as he pulled her tight, while carefully holding his framed drawing.

"What a great reunion!" said George, as he entered the store. "Welcome back, Mr. Celebrity," he added, as he shook hands with Karl. "Your fame grows, but I'll let Karla tell you all about that.

"Karla, it's close to quitting time," said George, with a smile. "Why don't you take the rest of the day off."

"Thanks, I will, gladly," said Karla.

"Before we go, let me show you something," said Karl, as he held out the drawing.

"Well, what do you know!" exclaimed George, as Karla looked on, "Inscribed and signed by Frank Lloyd Wright himself. So you finally met him!"

"Yup, at lunch today," said Karl, "and look at all the other signatures on the back! They even had a special cake for me…and lots of encouragement to come back soon."

"Come on, Karl," said Karla, as she took him by the hand. "Lets show this to Kirsten. She'll be so pleased."

"Yeah, Uncle Bill was impressed when I showed it to him," said Karl.

Art Sleuths

When they got close to the Nelsons', they spotted Anja and Ingrid, who came running to Karl.

"We finished the tennis lesson," said Anja, "and Ingrid thought you might be home soon."

Kirsten came out the door, and hugged Karl and exclaimed, "Welcome back, Karl. It seems like you've been gone a long time. Come on in, all of you, and celebrate with cake and coffee!"

As they enjoyed the treat, Karl showed the framed drawing to Kirsten, Anja and Ingrid.

"They had a great farewell lunch for me at Taliesin," explained Karl, "and Mr. Wright was there to greet me and thank me for helping at Taliesin. And he gave me one of his drawings. And look at all those signatures on the back!"

"You've earned a lot more recognition here, too," said Kirsten.

With that opening, they all reported about Karl's spreading fame.

"That radio program really did it," said Anja. "Imagine, an art show described on the radio! The listeners really responded, and your exhibit has been busy every day since you've been gone."

As Anja was leaving, she asked, "Would you two like to go along with Dan and me to see the movie in the park tonight? Don't know what the movie might be, but it would be fun."

"That does sound like fun," said Karla.

"Sounds like fun to me," said Karl, "but what about her beau in Madison?" he quietly asked Anja.

"I think she's disappointed and disgusted with her 'one-and-only'," said Anja. "He didn't get here all summer, and he only wrote to complain after he heard Karla on the radio praising your paintings."

"How did he stake out a claim on her?" asked Karl.

"He spotted her among freshmen interested in student government. As a self-important member of the student senate, he zeroed in on a vulnerable and a good-looking freshman. Understandably, she was flattered by the attention from a big man on campus and was caught in his web. Now she's beginning to see the light!"

Later, Karl shared his mixed feelings with Karla. "Anja told me about your frustration with your boyfriend. Sorry if I messed up your relationship," said Karl.

"Don't be," said Karla, as she touched his hand. "I know I'll enjoy being with you."

That evening, as the four of them sat on a bench in the park, eating popcorn brought by Anja, watching fireflies and swatting at mosquitoes, they talked about the start of college.

"Sure would like to see you in a game, Dan," said Karl. "Not much chance, so we'll just have to get a report from you, Anja."

"Are you going to be in a dorm or fraternity, Karl?" asked Dan.

"Neither. The arts department arranged for me to stay in the Lutheran Student Center," said Karl, "and they have reasonable room and board. Should be a great community."

"I should say so!" said Anja. "Guess who else will be living there."

As Karla smiled at Karl, he put his arm around her and squeezed. "Yup, me, all right," said Karla, as she leaned into Karl.

"Super!" said Karl. "You'll be handy for advice…and comforting when I need it, I hope."

They held hands during the Western and on the way to the Karla's.

"See you in church tomorrow," said Anja, as she and Dan went to her house. "All the students heading for college will be recognized. Should be a comforting send-off."

At her house, Karla asked, "Enjoy the movie?"

"I don't really remember the movie," said Karl, "but I sure enjoyed being with you. I guess I won't even have to arm-wrestle your poetic boyfriend for the privilege."

As she hugged him, he placed his hand gently on the side of her face to kiss her.

"On our first date?" she said, with a smile.

"I guess it is, at that," he said.

"But, yes," she said as she kissed him.

After a final hug and kiss, she hurried into her house, saying, "See you tomorrow morning."

"Ummm…yes," he answered, in a daze.

Chapter 6: ON WISCONSIN! THE UNIVERSITY, THE YEAR 1938

At the request of George, Karl dropped by THE BREV in honor of Karla's last day there.

"I arranged for delivery of three malts so we could celebrate our special summer," said George, "and send both of you off to college.

"I'll miss you, and look forward to seeing you when you come home," continued George, between sips of his malt. "You made life interesting, both of you, especially as you teamed up with me and others on your remarkable art exhibit, Karl. Thanks to both of you, also, for joining me in the presentation about that event at the Chamber of Commerce. I think Charlie and others there are still stunned—and pleased—by that amazing event.

"So, here's to both of you," continued George, while he raised his metal malt container as a toast, and Karl and Karla followed suit.

"Now, I'm curious about your coming school year," he added. "What's on your agenda, Karla?"

"Maybe you heard, but, coincidentally, Karl and I will both live in the Lutheran Student Center."

"Roommates?" asked George, with a grin.

"No such luck," said Karl, with a smile.

"We'll also have some classes together," said Karla. "Working here helped interest me in graphic design, so we'll both take that course."

"The Taliesin experience and learning more about the Bauhaus opened my eyes to the developing field of graphic design, so we should enjoy learning together. Of course, Karla already works in graphic design," said Karl as he held up the Nelson cap marked with the saw and name.

"I'll get to try my hand and learn more about graphic design by part-time work for the arts department. Maybe even do some illustrations for the athletics department," said Karl.

"By the way, our art exhibit and my work at Taliesin have paid off at the University, because the arts department has placed me in an accelerated course of study," explained Karl.

"So we'll be together in another way, because Karl will start as a sophomore, based on interviews and tests and his portfolio of art," said Karla, with pride in her voice.

"I'll need Karla's help in another class we'll share," said Karl. "That's history of art. I guess I've been so busy painting that I haven't looked much at the past. But she's a whiz, and I'm benefiting already from her tutoring."

"For my language requirement, I plan to study Swedish that's offered as part of the Scandinavian Studies Program at the University. Might be interesting to be more involved in my heritage. But Karla decided against that. Makes me think she must be Norwegian," as he laughed, and so did she.

"Another place we won't be together is the Reserve Officers' Training Corps," asserted Karla.

"I figured the conflict in Europe might soon involve the United States," explained Karl, "so I decided I might as well get prepared by joining the ROTC. Besides, I'll earn some money that way, too."

Chapter 7: ATTACK ON CAMPUS

Karl hadn't expected conflict at the University. But it surfaced in the form of Harlan Hollister, who didn't accept the reality that Karla was his *former* girlfriend.

"I wondered if we would meet sometime," said Karl, when Harlan accosted him at the entrance of the Lutheran Center.

"Oh yes, I heard about you," said Harlan, "and I've seen how you cozy up to Karla. So I tell you now to cease and desist. If not, you might learn about the power I have on campus, and in my fraternity."

"I guess that would be up to Karla," said Karl.

"Nonsense! You seduced her during the summer, and I aim to get her out of your clutches," said Harlan. "For Christ's sake, a dumb Swede sailor cutting in on me! So back off, you bastard!"

"Or you'll send your Chicago thugs to teach me?" said Karl.

"You're getting the message," said Harlan.

Karl didn't mention the incident to Karla, and he didn't want to involve the Center or University officials, because he assumed Harlan was just blustering.

He did mention the threat to Jim Johnson, an acquaintance in the graphics class and also a reporter for the University newspaper.

"Can this be for real?" asked Karl after he explained the situation.

"That little Communist asshole thinks he's a big man on campus. His father is a left-leaning political science professor, so Harlan milked that connection and his fraternity to get elected to the student government.

"He seems motivated by the short guy's Napoleon complex, so taking on a big guy like you might appeal to him. Never know about a twerp like that. So watch your back."

After Karl had dismissed Harlan's warning as an idle threat, he learned the hard way the reality of the threat. Late one night in a dark area of the campus, he walked complacently on his way back to the Lutheran Center, until suddenly an attacker with a baseball bat clubbed him from behind. Then, while one assailant stood over him with the bat, two others pounded on him.

"Meet the Chicago thugs from my fraternity," scoffed Harlan. "I guess you didn't hear my message after all. Hope it got through to you this time!"

At the Lutheran Center, two other residents saw him stagger in and grabbed him.

"You look like you need a doctor," said one.

"Just need to be cleaned up," said Karl.

Then the other Samaritan tracked down Karla. Soon others came out of their rooms.

"Take him to the kitchen so we can see him in brighter light," said Karla.

She and others began to clean him up.

"No serious cuts, but you'll have black eyes and a few other bruises," said Karla.

"Oww! That's a big knob on my head," said Karl, as he felt where the bat had hit him.

"Let's get you comfortable in the lounge," said Karla, "and I'll stay with you to make sure you don't have a concussion. An ice pack on your head might reduce that bump."

"I'll call security," said one in the group.

"And I'll give a little quiz," said Karla, with a restrained smile.

"What's your name?" she asked.

After his correct response, she told him to look at her hand. "How many fingers do you see?"

"What fingers," he said with a laugh.

"Not a laughing matter," she scolded.

"Okay, four," he said. "For me to hold."

"I think he's functioning," came a restrained laugh from another helper.

"I'll let him rest on the couch and keep an eye on him till security shows up," said Karla.

When a man and woman from security arrived, they checked his responses, too, and gave him a passing grade—but warned him he would feel the pain for several days.

Next, they asked what had happened and who struck him. And they learned that he had not been robbed.

"I recall being hit and going down and trying to fight off some attackers. Then some muffled comments.

"I know who threatened me earlier, but I can't connect that positively to the incident," concluded Karl.

The security team left with a promise to investigate. "But don't count on any results, because it seems to have been a planned sneak attack with no witnesses and no evidence. At least not so far."

In the morning, Karla wondered why the attack had occurred, but Karl urged her not to get involved, or she might be hurt, too. For the time being, she settled for just helping him function.

But at the graphics class, Jim immediately declared he would push the paper to investigate. "At least we have a pretty good idea who attacked you, but proving it will be a challenge."

"The security office recorded the time and location of the attack...also the extent of my injuries. And noted my muddled comments, I'm told."

After much sympathy from faculty and students and his friends at the Center ,Karl shared a comment attributed to Abraham Lincoln about the reaction of a man tarred and feathered and run out of town: "If it weren't for the honor, I believe I'd rather have walked home without the attention of that gauntlet."

Art Sleuths

Fellow cadets in the ROTC offered to accompany Karl around campus, when they were available, as an honor guard.

In the athletics department, where Karl was completing a series of semi-realistic posters about football, his acquaintances on the team volunteered to be vigilantes.

"You said you were threatened by thugs from Chicago," said one. "I'm from Milwaukee. Let me know if you need help," said a muscular lineman from the team.

Karl laughed at the offer. "After practice, you look worse than I do, like you've been attacked."

"I have," he laughed. "There's no mercy out on the field. Even from my so-called friends on the team."

Memory of the attack faded as Karl immersed himself in the courses.

In studying the Vikings, he realized their difficulties and dangers far exceeded his challenges on the Great Lakes boats. He puzzled about the contrast of their aggressiveness and the peaceful people of Scandinavia now.

He also found the runic symbols of early writings in Scandinavia to be intriguing as a form of communication...and as interesting graphic design.

Graphic design and the history of art inspired both Karl and Karla as part of their intellectual and romantic enjoyment of each other. The accomplishments of both caught the attention of the instructors, who asked them to tell about their involvement in graphics.

Karla showed examples of designs she had created for businesses in Richland Center, including the "saw & Nelson" symbol as shown on the cap worn by Karl. And she showed some of her designs being used by the student newspaper and by the Lutheran Student Center.

For his report, Karl displayed and described some of his paintings, and Karla provided a dramatic story about the unusual exhibit. "Amazingly, a radio station from here in Madison decided to broadcast that art show, and it proved to be a big hit!"

"I like your new sports painting," said another friend from the Lutheran Center. "You seem to pick appealing subjects," he added, with a smile.

"Guess you know who this is," said Karl, proudly. "Karla had to put on her skiing gear…on a hot day way ahead of the season.

"She protested, but the others on her ski team love the result," grinned Karl. "So do I. And so does the sports information department, which will feature her on the cover of the booklet about the ski squad."

A painting marked "sold" shocked one student. "You actually sold a painting in these tough times!" she exclaimed.

The instructor in Karl's beginning architectural studies knew about and mentioned Karl's work at Taliesin. So the students 'demanded' to hear from Karl about his experience there. With obvious pride, he also told about being thanked by Frank Lloyd Wright for his contributions during that time.

Spiritual stimulation at the Lutheran Student Center and the fellowship there enriched the lives of the residents and the many visitors.

Karl's friend Jim Johnson, a Lutheran from Eau Claire, became a regular visitor, partly because of his special friendship with Ulrika Lindskog, another resident of the Center. And he brought others along to share the enjoyment of the convivial community.

One evening, he confided to Karl that the "dam is about to bust," because the newspaper "had the goods" on Harlan about the attack. "Be ready to share some thoughts, because another reporter might be in touch before the story is finalized."

On campus, with classes winding down and students savoring the successful season for the Wisconsin Badgers, quiet prevailed. For the Thanksgiving break, Karla and Karl caught a ride to Richland Center from two students heading to Stevens Point. Though Karl wasn't able to return home for the holiday, he told his parents that he and Uncle Bill and family—and Karla—planned to journey to Superior for part of the Christmas vacation from the University.

On campus after the holiday, the student newspaper published a story that shook the entire University.

Below the headline, **STUDENT LEADER EXPELLED FOR ASSULT AND BATTERY,** the story revealed the vicious attack by senior Harlan Hollister on sophomore Karl Nelson.

Hollister, member of the student government and son of a prominent and vocal political science professor, led three others from his fraternity as they waylaid Nelson in a dark part of the campus a month ago. Struck by a baseball bat and beaten-on while he was down, Nelson staggered to his residence at the Lutheran Student Center.

Other residents there administered First Aid, and campus security responded to a call for help.

Members of the security team and this newspaper have joined in investigating the incident since it occurred.

Finally, the crime cover-up at the fraternity was exposed when another member of the fraternity, junior Francis Langton, provided details about the planning and conducting of the attack. He said he was "fed up" with the notoriety caused by others of the fraternity.

"Jealousy had put Harlan in a frenzy," said the student. "He's accustomed to getting what he wants, and the loss of a girlfriend to Nelson motivated the attack he led.

"Though he organized the attack, he didn't actually participate physically," said Langton. "He said Harlan considers himself a poet and doesn't stoop to that level of violence."

Others at the fraternity and on the student senate were less "poetic" in their descriptions of Hollister.

According to Nelson, Hollister earlier had called him a "dumb Swede" and threatened to "bring his Chicago thugs" to teach Nelson a lesson. At that time, Nelson had told reporter Jim Johnson about the threat, and Johnson had alerted the editor about Hollister's behavior.

After the announcement of Hollister's expulsion, Nelson expressed satisfaction that now the "lesson has been turned back on Hollister."

Because of the apparent intervention of the "poet's" father," Prof. Jefferson Hollister, no criminal charges have been lodged against his son. He declined comment on the advice of the family lawyer.

The University President, Dr. Kenneth Adams, declared that such a brutal attack cannot be tolerated, so the University administration acted appropriately in expelling Hollister. He anticipates no further punishment at this time.

The story shocked Karla. "Sorry you suffered that attack because of me!" she exclaimed apologetically.

"No," said Karl, "because of him. How could you know he would turn so vicious, and what could you have done about it anyway?"

"Well, I got a hint when he called to threaten me at the end of summer," said Karla. "But a 'poet' hardly seems the type to turn violent. Verbally abusive, yes, but not cause a physical attack."

"Well, I'm glad for your sake—and ours—that you got free of him," said Karl, as he wrapped his arms around Karla. "Fortunately, he didn't have his goons attack you."

"I'm certainly relieved that you're okay," said Karla, as she kissed Karl. "Thanks for your understanding, and for not mentioning my name in the incident."

That night, after the story spread in the media throughout the state and beyond, Karl and Karla both got calls from worried parents.

The parents expressed surprise and dismay about the incident, and they were all thankful Karl didn't suffer lasting injury.

"I guess I'm just a hard-headed Swede after all," laughed Karl.

Karla's father stated that the blow on the head, in particular, could have caused worse consequences.

"Your mother and I offered prayers of thanks for Karl's recovery, and we prayed for the continuing strength of your loving relationship," said Henrik to his daughter.

Meanwhile, the editor of the student newspaper wrote a scathing editorial, which media of the wider area picked up. Many papers and radio stations also noted that the victim of the attack on campus is the artist honored last summer by the town of Richland Center.

In support of the heading **AMBUSH BY STUDENTS TARNISHES WISCONSIN IMAGE,** the editor wrote:

For a state and university considered "progressive," our reputation was smeared by a recent sadistic ambush of a student on campus.

Ironically, the brutal attack in the dark and from behind was led by Harlan Hollister, who had been a member of the student senate and considers himself a socialist espousing fairness to all.

As further irony, his father, Political Science Professor Jefferson Hollister, frequently lambastes Adolf Hitler for that kind of lawlessness. In contrast, because of his own left-leaning convictions, he often excuses similar behavior by Josef Stalin.

Evidently, his "above-it-all" son and "poet" Harlan favors "flexible" judgment of individuals and feels he has a right to express his anger as he chooses. Like Hitler, he even resorts to ethnic slurs, in this case calling his victim, Karl Nelson, a "dumb Swede."

Personally, this editor takes umbrage at that comment, as no doubt thousands of other Swedes at the University and in the state do as well.

In another bit of irony, the insulted victim comes from the city of—Superior.

Now a degree of justice has been served, with the expulsion of Hollister and his collaborators.

My personal apology goes to Nelson, and my thanks go to the investigative staff of this newspaper and the Security Department of the University for solving this brutal and unwarranted attack.

Chapter 8: HOLIDAY RESPITE

When the Christmas vacation began, Henrick and Elin drove to Madison to pick up Karla and Karl. Then they all headed to Superior to share Christmas with Karl's parents.

Bengt and Tina welcomed the Lindholms warmly, with regret for not meeting them in Richland Center.

"Because of Karl's letters, even if they were few and far between, we feel like we're old friends," said Tina. "Of course, Karla seems like a daughter to us, after Karl's loving comments. Thanks also for your call to comfort us when the news about Karl's injury came to light."

The friendship blossomed during meals and while shopping in Duluth. There the Lindholms saw the docks and ships where Karl worked and where Bengt has been based for many years. On the way home, they drove by the high school where Tina teaches, and where Karl had participated in so many ways.

"Sorry we didn't have time for skiing," said Karl. "I know you're an expert, and I hoped to get some pointers from you."

"I'm no expert, but I did make the ski team," said Karla, "and I do enjoy skiing and skating in the winter, and tennis and swimming in the summer. Keeps me in shape."

"Yeah, I like that shape," grinned Karl.

Then the Christmas worship, the fellowship at the Lutheran church afterward, and the Christmas dinner at the Nelsons provided a fitting conclusion to that holiday.

On New Year's Day in Richland Center, the Chamber of Commerce sponsored a quieter continuation of the celebration of the night before.

Besides providing an indoor picnic in the City Hall, the C of C again honored Karl and Karla.

"You sure seem to be getting a lot attention for our little community," said Charlie. "I'm sure sorry the sensational recent news had to come from a bonk on the head for you, Karl.

"But we remember you most for your dramatic display of art," continued Charlie, "and from what we hear from Madison, you and Karla continue to get lots of recognition for your ongoing involvement at the University.

"So we say 'welcome home!' and 'bon voyage' as you head back to the University. May it be safer the rest of the school year for you."

Others from the community stopped by to chat, and finally George got a chance to talk with them. "I'm sure pleased to learn of your continuing involvement in art, because I see so much potential for both of you."

Ted and two others from Taliesin waited for an opportunity to compare notes. "More wanted to come," laughed Ted, "but they didn't want to ride alfresco in this weather. So I squeezed these two in the cab with me."

"I'm pleased to see you guys again, especially after I've been telling the students and instructors about my enriching experience at Taliesin," said Karl. "I hope I haven't exaggerated my association with you, but everyone seems highly curious and eager to hear about my humble participation there."

"Don't let a bit exaggeration stop you, because everything at Taliesin seems like a bit of exaggeration," grinned Hal Harchan. "But the environment continues to be stimulating in its own exaggerated way.

"Here are some more tidbits to share with your eager audience," continued Hal, as he listed projects on the drawing board, some actually in construction and a few in the wild imaginings.

"Hope you can come back in the summer," said Ted. "I get lonesome without you."

"I think I'm supposed to be plying my graphics for the arts department communication and for the athletics department," said Karl. "But I'll try to drop in when I can."

"And bring lovely Karla, too," said Ted.

The remainder of the school year seemed calm and anticlimactic after the first semester, and both Karl and Karla continued to excel in their studies and advance in their "on-the-job" application of graphic design.

Karl particularly thanked Karla for sharing her considerable knowledge of the history of art.

As they explored the Renaissance with others from the Center, Karl marveled both at the talent of those times and the politics affecting the arts and architecture then.

In the ROTC program, Col. Haaken Hansen singled out Karl and a few others for extra training in the science of cryptography. He commended Karl's curiosity about languages, and he encouraged Karl as he explored the runic characters used in the lands of the early Nordics.

To those selected for the special work in cryptography, he explained that leaders of the United States downplayed the need for counter-intelligence capability.

"One of our political leaders even excused that," he said, "by declaring 'We don't read our neighbors' mail.'

"Consequently," he continued, "we're just scratching the surface, while Germany and the Soviet Union, and even the British, have been spying on us very effectively.

"Well, we don't need the President's approval for what we're doing," he added, "so let's keep at it. The storm clouds of Europe are growing darker and darker!"

"But I sure wonder what goes on behind all the bombasts from the German Bund," said Col. Hansen. "Might there be German spies lurking behind that noisy blather?"

"Well," said Karl, after he thought about the question, "my friend on the football team, Hank Schmidt, berates his German ancestry because of the war and now because of Hitler. He said his family has suffered from some resentment because of the war.

"He is from Milwaukee, and that's the heart of the Bund, isn't it?"

"Sure is!"

"Maybe he could do some snooping for us," said Karl.

"If he's interested, bring him by," said Col. Hansen.

Karl shared with Karla his feelings about the benefits of the ROTC. "I'm learning a lot about leadership—for life, not just for the military.

"I hope you get a chance to meet Col. Hansen some day. He's become like a big brother to me. In fact, we should have you in our discussion about trends in Scandinavia. He thinks his relatives in Norway made a big mistake in separating from Sweden, just at a time when they need the strength of unity.

"Denmark wouldn't have a chance if Germany should attack," said Karl. "In less than a century, they already lost half of their land to Germany.

"And then there's Finland, caught between the grip of the Soviet Union and the ambitions of Germany.

"Col. Hansen urged me to keep up on my Swedish, because he thinks that could be important location in case the United States ever needs to establish a counter-intelligence activity in Europe."

"That's a bleak picture," said Karla. "What do you and the others in ROTC predict?"

"We think war in Europe might explode soon," said Karl. "Our biggest concern is whether United States will get involved.

"That's showing up literally right here," added Karl. "Dad is now working on plans to protect the shipping in the Great Lakes. He and others worry particularly about the Soo Locks at Saulte Ste. Marie, which are vital and vulnerable. You can imagine the impact if sabotage cut into the shipments of iron ore, not to mention oil and grain."

Summer brightened the outlook for both Karl and Karla, as they continued to live at the Lutheran Student Center and provide graphics as part of their work for the University. Sometimes they teamed up on projects, which they both found enjoyable and educational.

Their occasional visits to Richland Center included some interesting and educational time at Taliesin. And they checked in with George at THE BREV, followed by their traditional malt at the soda fountain next door.

Bengt and Tina came down from Superior in their motor home, and the Nelson family reunion involved several other unofficial parts of the clan from the church and community.

Karl and Karla welcomed the opportunity to take in an outdoor movie with Dan and Anja— alongside the fireflies and mosquitoes. Before the movie, they shared stories of college life, including the ambush of Karl. After the "show on the grass," they got together with others from the church for refreshments at the Lindholms'.

Chapter 9: WAR WORRIES IN THE UNITED STATES

At the start of the school year in 1939, Germany's invasion of Poland ended speculation about war, as Great Britain and France responded in support of their pact with Poland.

Soon, a desperate Britain needed help from the neutral United States, which responded with unofficial support of the British war effort by the creation of a special "lend-lease" provision for the virtual donation of ships and supplies.

The University campus remained calm but tense, as the male faculty, staff and students in particular kept a wary eye on the trends in Europe. Denmark and Norway fell quickly to the onslaught of the Nazi invasion early in 1940. Then the German Blitzkrieg shifted to The Netherlands, Belgium, Luxembourg and France.

Americans learned with horror about some 300,000 British soldiers trapped at Dunkirk on the English Channel, but then felt restrained relief when British ships and boats of all sizes conducted an amazing rescue in May of 1940.

ROTC activity at the University intensified, and Karl took on additional leadership responsibilities as part of a new emphasis on counter-intelligence. Initially, he and a few others from the Wisconsin ROTC took further training at a nearby Army base, but then the Army's new Special Operations Command requested that Col. Hansen and his cryptography unit take part in concentrated study at Fort Bragg in North Carolina

With Karl at the beck and call of the ROTC and the Army, the happy, romantic companionship of Karl and Karla also experienced dramatic disruption.

Karla worried continually about Karl and their future, with the United States on the verge of war.

"At least," laughed Karl, as he hugged Karla, "we have great 'goodbyes' and exciting reunions."

Their families, and many other families and friends of the men at the University, stayed on edge with worry as the war intensified in Europe. At the

Lutheran Center, the strife in Europe dominated student gatherings.

In Richland Center, a committee involving the Chamber of Commerce, the newspaper and the high school hosted periodic meetings for the public at City Hall. The committee invited Karl and Karla to participate in the forum when they were available.

Karla had taken a strong personal interest in her World History course, so she provided insights about the current world tensions. The punishment of Germany after the "war to end all wars" fueled their current aggression, she explained, and the League of Nations has turned into hollow idealism. In frustration, some leaders had advocated unification of Scandinavia and other democracies of the North Atlantic for self-defense. But German aggression and growing isolationism shot that down, she added.

Karl shared as much as appropriate about the changing role of the ROTC.

When Bengt and Tina visited Richland Center, the committee asked Bengt for an overview about defense preparations in Great Lakes shipping.

With the start of the new school year of 1940, Col. Hansen requested a meeting with Karl and the others in the cryptography unit.

"I know I can't order your participation in what I'm about to explain," he said, "but I truly believe in the importance of a special assignment for us in a new quasi-military unit.

"Besides," he laughed in a grim way, "you would likely be drafted into the regular Army in a short time, the way the war is unfolding. Not an appealing alternative, if you ask me.

"Anyway, those of you who are willing to accompany me to England will be able to continue your college work at Cambridge and at the same time learn how we can work with the British intelligence organization. Believe me, they are far ahead of us in that activity. Also, the new British Commandos will see that you stay fit and become ready for combat.

"Because our country remains neutral, you will be officially classified as visiting students.

"By the way, the University of Wisconsin will grant your degree just the same as if you finished here. Of course, going to Cambridge will be quite an honor in itself."

Many of last semester's students were back at the Lutheran Student Center, so those friends of Karl and the new residents wished him bon voyage in a somber celebration.

They realized, as did Karla, that Karl could be gone for months, even years, depending on the intensity of fighting in Europe—and if and when the United States might also declare war on the Axis powers.

During their emotional final days, Karl and Karla reluctantly agreed that marriage and even engagement would not be desirable. And Karl urged Karla not to become a recluse. "You have lots of interesting friends—male as well as female— including several interested in the arts as well as sports. So I hope you will feel free to expand your social life.

"Well, not too quickly," he smiled. "And don't include Harlan."

"I don't know how I'll get along without you," she said, with tears flowing. "We've meant so much to each other."

Holding his hand, she led him to the room she occupied alone as a resident leader.

Kissing him desperately, she murmured, "I need to have you with me!"

Soon they were locked in urgent intercourse, as they shared soft cries and groans.

"Now I can remember us as one," she sobbed.

"This will help make our separation bearable," he declared softly. "This was wonderful!

"I'll hurry back—whenever that might be, depending on Germany's expanding aggression. I'll write as often as I can. But I might have to censor my own letters, because that will be a responsibility of our cryptography unit," he added, with a slight smile.

Chapter 10: CAMBRIDGE, ENGLAND, THE YEAR 1940

By mid-September, Col. Hansen—now referred to as the teacher—and his six "students" quietly went north to Winnipeg to join a Canadian unit flying to Britain.

"We'll be landing at an airbase near the small town of Duxford," explained Col. Hansen, "which, by the way, borders Cambridge University. We'll enroll you there as part of your training. Not bad, I'd say!"

On the plane, they all quickly developed friendships, partly because all realized they would be "second-class citizens" in Britain.

"Yeah, just outlanders from the Colonies," laughed Karl. "But I believe we will live in the part of England the Vikings conquered more than a thousand years ago. I should feel right at home," he laughed.

"Right now," said a grim Col. Hansen, "I think the Brits are in a state of shock. As Churchill predicted a couple of months ago, the Battle of France is over and the Battle of Britain will be next. Now the air battle is in full force, from all we hear."

"Yeah, I believe the Canucks and Yanks will be more than welcome," said one of the Canadians. "I hope we can do some good."

By the end of October, the Battle of Britain seemed to be winding down, as the British experts puzzled about why. Was Hitler frustrated by the resistance? Did he want to save his force for other targets? Or did he still hope Britain would decide to become an ally against the Communism of the Soviet Union?

Before long, Cambridge stimulated and challenged Karl mentally, and the Commando training tested and prepared him physically.

At the same time, the British intelligence organization began to involve the Americans students in their system. The British leaders soon learned that they had to teach the friendly and trusting Americans to be constantly on guard, because the German spies—men and women—were skilled at gathering information.

When another student at Cambridge learned of Karl's interest in art and architecture, he arranged a trip to see the British Museum in London.

"We'd better make a run for it, now that the air war has apparently subsided," he urged. "You never know if that museum will even survive the war."

The huge museum, with its multiple buildings, amazed and intrigued Karl.

"Just think," he shared with his friend and guide, "this began even before the United States was a country. And it opened a century before our magnificent Metropolitan Museum in New York began. "

"That was when the sun never set on the Union Jack," said Laurence. "So precious art and artifacts and documents and books funneled in from all over the empire, and British collectors were branching out beyond that. Even to America."

After a full day at the museum, Laurence recommended saving more for later. "The brain, and the feet, can only take so much of this. Besides, now that you have a general idea of the contents, we can explore much more just in discussions at Cambridge. We have lots of experts there."

Later, Laurence offered another idea: "I'd like to take you to meet Henry Holter. He's retired on a farm not far from where you live in Duxford, and he taught art history at Cambridge for years and years. Besides, you'd enjoy seeing him in action as a painter."

Several days later, Laurence arranged the meeting, and Henry and Karl soon found that their interests and personalities blended comfortably. So, before long, Karl became a weekend fixture at Henry's studio, where he resumed painting and gained from the mentoring by Henry. In turn, Henry was eager to learn about Karl's experience at Taliesin and about the special show of Karl's art.

"I sure was lucky in getting such support," said Karl, "just as I am now in getting help from you. The last I heard, my art sponsor in Wisconsin created a traveling exhibit of my crazy collection.

My paints made from iron ore and from dyes like those of the Indians evidently have caught a lot of attention."

Karl shared samplings of his new knowledge and associations in his letter to Karla:

Dearest Karla,

I think of you constantly, and miss you every time I have a free moment. And I'm continually thankful for our union before I left.

Now I have special art activities that relate directly to you. As I experience these new learning opportunities, I almost feel like you are here and sharing with me.

A British friend at Cambridge has taken me under his wing in connecting me with the British Museum and a variety of art galleries. After hearing my (our) great interest in art, he recently introduced me to a retired Cambridge art history professor who operates his rural studio not far from our quarters.

Now I visit him every weekend I'm free, and I am soaking up so much interesting information. He's an outstanding artist himself, and he has been very interested in my art. He finds our love and shared interests heartwarming, and he hopes to get acquainted with you also in the future.

I raised a question here about the fairness of countries such as Britain collecting art from all over the world. In the British empire, does might make right, both in national power and individual wealth, in acquiring art from Egypt and Greece and many other countries? Even in Sweden, Anders Zorn began collecting art from other countries after he achieved financial success. One justification for

Britain—the art will be preserved for the benefit of all. Napoleon and earlier military leaders felt conquering included art. Well, President Andrew Jackson started a trend in the United States with his belief that the victor deserves the spoils. So does that justify the Nazis' taking art from the Jews of Germany, for instance? And did those wealthy Jews create or just acquire art?

That has stimulated interesting discussions at Cambridge and with my retired professor. I'll keep you informed about the trend of the dialogue.

Meanwhile, the war affects us continually, though the air war that Churchill labeled the Battle of Britain seems to be tapering off. The reason for Hitler's backing off puzzles many here, and the country seems to be waiting for the other shoe to drop, so to speak.

I can't say much about our special training here. Our own cryptography unit would censor anything related to the war, anyway.

Mail doesn't move quickly, because our censors even scrutinized your recent letter. German espionage seems to prevail in every way. But I certainly relished your loving thoughts (hope the censors did, too) and the interesting news from our families and from the University.

Your preparations for skiing competition must be rigorous, by what you explained. Maybe like my regimen in the physical training I've been assigned to. Congratulations on making the ski team, and I look forward to the results of your events. And I will try to visualize you in the downhill skiing. Maybe I can paint that scene to serve as a current reminder of you.

*With the moderate climate here, I find it hard
to realize that snow will soon be flying in Wisconsin,
if it hasn't already.*

*I hope I've couched my thoughts in a way that
won't get the attention of the censors. However, we
have been warned that German women spies might
even ply us students for information. Maybe even by
sending us letters. So, I now remind the censors that
you are Scandinavian, not German, even though you
are from Wisconsin.*

*Please pass along my brief thoughts to our
families and friends.*

*And I pass along to you my love for you. And I
promise to save up my growing knowledge about art
to share with you. And my love to share with you.
What a joy that will be.*

With love from Karl

Friends at Cambridge as well as Henry Holter,
and a few other American nationals in the area,
helped make Christmas meaningful. But the holiday
hit Karl hard, as he thought about his family and
friends gathering in Richland Center to celebrate
Christmas.

But before the end of the year, the pace and
purpose of Karl's studies changed dramatically. Col.
Hansen alerted him that he was needed for a special
assignment, and he asked Karl to participate in a
meeting with leaders of the British intelligence
service.

"We need to plant you in Sweden while you
can still be considered a civilian," said the British
leader. "With your fluent Swedish, and even your
Swedish heritage, we feel we can connect you with
the Swedish university system."

"When will that occur?" asked Karl.

"Just as soon as we put you through intense training in the handling of the radio and in other aspects of intelligence work, as well as defining for you what we want to know and what we want to happen," said the British leader. "Evidently, your athletic ability helped you get outstanding marks in your work with the Commandos, but we hope that training won't be critical to your undercover work. However, it could save your life some day. I hope you aren't queasy about flying, because you will soon get training to enable you to fly a small plane. And here's a thrill," said the leader, with a smile, "you'll learn how to parachute from a plane, as well. Once again, we hope that won't be necessary later, but just in case."

During the next few days, Karl endured rigors that even exceeded his sailing in the winter on the Great Lakes. And the mental challenges more than matched the classes at the University.

He learned that he would be a visiting student at Lund University, located in southern Sweden, where he could gather intelligence about shipping from Sweden to Germany. Also, from there, he would be able to connect with underground activities in Denmark, Norway, Finland and the Baltic countries.

Karl also learned that he would be walking a fine line, because if Sweden learned of his "extracurricular" activities, he might end up imprisoned there. Or deported. Either, he was reminded, would cause a major setback to the intelligence operations.

Chapter 11: SHOCK FROM HOME

"What terrible news!" said one of the cryptographers from the Wisconsin unit as he censored incoming mail. "How will we ever be able to share this with Karl?" he continued in anguish. "Wish this wasn't part of our duty!"

"Let me get Col. Hansen," said another, after reading the letter.

When Col. Hansen arrived, they explained that a letter to Karl from his mother contained news of a tragedy involving Karl's girlfriend. "She died in a bus accident."

Col. Hansen read the letter that told about a bus with a University of Wisconsin ski team skidded on ice into a farm tractor crossing the ice-covered road.

He shared aloud the details about how the bus driver had tried to avoid the tractor, but the front corner of the bus where Karla sat caught the impact of the collision. She and the tractor driver were killed instantly, and several others on the bus were seriously injured.

"I'll meet with Karl to tell him the tragic news before he reads the letter," said Col. Hansen. "We can't even consider sending him home, because of the urgency of our activity. Besides, that wouldn't bring her back. But your extra support for him at this time will be appreciated, and we at least can arrange to send our condolences to Karl's family and Karla's family."

Karl's demanding training schedule helped him cope with much of his grief, and his cryptography associates and his British friends constantly offered support during his suffering.

Later, in his airborne training, he admitted that the tether to open his parachute saved his life in his first jump right after he received the tragic news. He explained that had the pulling of the ripcord been up to him at the time, he might have just gone into free fall all the way to the ground to join Karla in heaven.

Slowly, with the added challenge of Commando preparation, his despondency faded and his determination prevailed.

Chapter 12: LUND, SWEDEN, THE YEAR 1941

Early in 1941, Col. Hansen alerted Karl to be ready to drop in on his Swedish relatives. "Wish we could let you fly in on a small plane, but that might get too much attention over hostile territory. So you'll be parachuting in, and the Swedish military intelligence organization, C-byrån, will be there to meet you and set you up to carry out your assignments. A Swedish intelligence operative, who's a 'student' at Lund University, will guide you there and be your ongoing contact. Your involvement in art should provide you a good cover for 'exploring' a variety of unusual places.

"And, as an American citizen, you should be able to travel openly in Sweden. But you must be constantly on guard, considering you are part of an American military unit. And the Swedish intelligence organization has to walk a tight line to ensure Swedish neutrality. But once set up there, you can start your 'civilian' life as a student. You should even be able to contact your own relatives, because that would be logical for an American visitor. But be watchful.

"And don't break a leg in landing!" he laughed, with grim humor.

Karl and his "fellow student" at Lund, Major Kjell Seastrand, bonded quickly, despite the tradition of Swedish reserve.

"I like your name, 'shell at the sea shore,' so that should be easy to remember," said Karl.

"Good analysis, and an interesting way of saying my name, with an American twist to it," laughed Kjell. "Now, let me set the stage for your 'graduate study' at Lund.

"You'll be living in a student apartment building, in your own room, because you'll be employed as a maintenance person there. We heard you have a good mix of skills, so this will make a convincing case for you to earn your way. Also, your job will give you plenty of opportunity to be out in the community and beyond, as you get supplies for the building and shop for hardware to make any repairs needed.

"You'll have tools to service your radio as well. And, by the way, you'll be working for our intelligence agency besides yours. We have a major stake in this too. And, from what we've heard about the intelligence activity by the United States, you lag far behind others. But so do we, so we're eager to use your skills and connections. Don't worry, though, because our agency will keep that very quiet.

"So let's take a tour to orient you," said Kjell.

The tour began at the apartment building, where Karl saw his apartment, including a kitchen.

"You can get meals at the University or eat here," said Kjell. "But I hope you won't starve on your own cooking.

"We installed your radio in the closet, behind that panel that looks like part of the wall," added Kjell.

"Guess I'll look American," laughed Karl, as he examined the working attire, as well as casual clothes.

"Because you're American and because of your job," explained Kjell, "you can dress unconventionally for Sweden. Makes you look, shall we say, unsophisticated."

They chatted about life in the university community, as Kjell led the way to the buildings most important to Karl.

Kjell explained that his own studies were in engineering, in another part of the campus.

"Here's a place we both will use regularly— the shop for us engineers and for art students like you who want to do some welding," said Kjell, as they entered a well-equipped workshop.

"I won't try to meet with you on any schedule, just run into you as we cross paths," said Kjell. "But here's a place we can leave messages for the time being," he added, as he pressed a concealed button and raised top of a tool cabinet to reveal a shallow space. "It's big enough for a note but not large enough to be noticed.

"Later, with your radio, you can contact Haaken and me, even record a message," said Kjell. "And your radio receiver records as well.

"We've provided you with maps, including the layout of the campus, so I'll let you wander around to get your bearings. The building where you will have most of your art classes and discussion groups is over there," concluded Kjell.

"Well, I'm on my way to adjusting to this strange new life," said Karl. "Thanks so much," he said as he shook hands. "I hope this war doesn't cause a disaster here."

Karl's first class—or gathering—startled him. When he entered the room, the instructor shook hands and suggested a place where Karl could sit at the end of the semicircle of a dozen graduate students, seven men and five women.

"I'm Dr. Lars Johansson," he said in English, as he addressed Karl, "and this is an advanced study of Art History. We're pleased to have you here to add a perspective from America. We've read about you, so we already know you as Karl Nelson from Wisconsin, USA.

"At this stage of our study, we are considering the wide range of art materials used over the years. From what we've read, we learned that you've employed some interesting materials, so we are eager to learn more. But first, I'll ask the students to introduce themselves and add anything that might be of interest to you."

Each in order stood to give name and home location. Most said little more, but two mentioned relatives in America, and Karl responded that he knew of those places. One woman, the last to introduce herself, explained that she had studied at the Art Academy in Minneapolis, and Karl acknowledged that he lived near there.

Then she added: "I read that you learned some of your paint colors from the Indians. That sounds interesting to me," she said, as the others, including the Dr. Johansson, waited with evident interest too.

Karl explained that some of the Ojibway Indians were his friends as well as classmates in school. He told of the dyes they had developed from plants, and how he had learned from them and tried the dyes in his own paintings.

"We also noticed your use of iron ore for paint," said another student. "We know about that because of the iron ore in Sweden."

"Yeah," smiled another, "you'll see lots of red buildings here because of that."

"Part of what we read indicated that you didn't use canvas, but some type of pressed wood," said the man next to him. "What is that and why did you use it?"

"Necessity was the reason," smiled Karl, as he told about salvaging his "canvases" from discarded panels used in shipping.

"I think we have that kind of panel in Sweden," said another, "but I never thought of it for painting."

"I'm not surprised that Sweden has developed that, too, because you're known for your forest products," said Karl. "I'd like to try it here, if you can help me find some."

Others nodded their heads, indicating their desire to experiment, too.

The instructor smiled and encouraged the dialogue during the rest of the session. When the class finished, he shook hands again with Karl, and all the students did as well.

After the class, Karl thought about "snooping" opportunities in connection with the history of art materials. *Besides papyrus, parchment and fabric, maybe we could add wood pulp, he speculated. That could be an interesting medium that would accept not only colors but also embossing, debossing and die-cutting. That could provide me an excuse to visit a pulp and paper mill in Sweden...and learn about the northern forests, the iron mines...and even try to get a line on the German transportation that is being allowed to cross Sweden.*

Before checking out lunch options, Karl decided first to look for an opportunity to try the welder he heard about in the University workshop.

There, as he got the familiar protective gear and examined the arc welder, he caught the impression of the flashing light and colors of another person already welding. Soon he was also creating a scene of light and color and smoke as he ran streams of molten metal on a flat plate.

When he flipped his mask up to check results, the other welder surprised him, standing beside him and raising the mask to examine his simple creation.

"Oh, hi!" he said. "I didn't recognize you in your welding outfit. But now I do recognize you from the class. You're Inge Lindfelt, aren't you?"

"Good memory!" she responded.

"Selective memory," he said, with a smile that was matched by hers.

"I see you've found another art medium," she said, "and you must like our Runic characters as an expression."

"I like the simplicity of the lines, and this bead of metal gives me the feel for the letters, you might say," he said, with a slight grin.

"You might," she smiled, "and I might, too."

"I'd like to get a better understanding of what they communicated," he added.

"I'll be glad to help," she said, "and some time we could look at the Runestone right here on the campus, as well as some others not far away."

"Would lunch time be a good time to take a look?" he asked. "I need to find a place to eat. So would you join me and show the way?"

"You Americans don't waste any time, do you?" she laughed. "I remember that from Minneapolis, too. A bit startling to a Swede."

"I take that as a yes," he responded.

"Why not," she said, "even if I'm the talk of the department. I believe this is called a 'pick up,' as I heard in Minneapolis."

"I've been told that I know how to pick 'em," he said. "My artistic eye."

During the nutritious lunch, featuring fruits and vegetables and multi-grain bread plus yogurt to drink, she told of her experiments with art and her hope to teach others. "I don't know how much welding I might teach," she laughed, "but I enjoy the challenge for myself."

As he was about to respond, a slight middle-aged man, meticulously attired, and authoritative in manner, interrupted them.

"Well, Miss Lindfelt," he said firmly, "I see that you didn't waste any time in promoting international relations.

"I gather that you are the American who will be studying in our department. I'm Professor Berghoff, and I understand you will be in our art group studying German art."

"I'm Karl Nelson, the American interloper," said Karl, "and I look forward to learning more about the impact of that art. Would you like to join us for lunch?"

"No, have to run," said the professor, "but this was an opportunity to welcome you. I, too, look forward to your participation in our class. You might offer an interesting perspective.

"You can brief him about what to expect, Miss Lindfelt, and I'll see both of you in class."

"That was a chilly introduction," said Karl after the professor left. "He seems more like what I think of as a stuffy Swede, in contrast to Dr. Johansson."

"You're right," said Inge, "they're like night and day. Dr. Johansson seems more like an American, and Dr. Berghoff seems more like an arrogant German. I'm his student assistant, and he tends to be rather possessive of me. I do believe he was a bit annoyed by my having lunch with you. I imagine he will enjoy challenging you...and me."

Later Karl learned that Dr. Johansson had worked his way up from a middle-class family in the Swedish education establishment, while Dr. Berghoff had capitalized on his aristocratic connections.

During the next few weeks, Karl fit in well with his fellow students. And Anders Carlson invited him to join in an informal gathering of students from a cross-section of the university.

"I believe you call that a 'mixer' in America," said Anders. "We just get together to 'hit the bull'," he added.

"That's really called 'shoot the bull'," said Karl, with a smile, "even if it doesn't make a lot of sense, and it probably can't be translated into Swedish. But, thanks, I welcome the opportunity."

Art Sleuths

When Karl joined the mix of students from disciplines such as economics, history, archeology, economics, engineering, medicine and sociology, he found the dynamics of the discussion to be stimulating.

The others, of course, wanted to know his perception of Sweden.

"Your country seems calm and steady, compared to the volatile nature of the United States," he explained in English. And he added, with a grin, "Maybe that's because the discontented Swedes left for America.

"Seriously," he added, "I learned that the loss of one-fourth of your population because of emigration led to major positive changes in Sweden."

Anders agreed, also in English: "For one thing, the emigration literally reduced the economic pressure here. But it also jolted our country into making changes to improve the quality of life in Sweden."

"I guess both countries benefited," said Karl, "because America gained a valuable infusion of people with ambition and integrity."

After more give and take, Karl thanked the others for including him, and they expressed appreciation for his insights.

In his apartment building, Karl got another view of Sweden from Johanna Svendal, who was glad to practice her English skills.

While he repaired her kitchen cabinets as part of his work responsibility, they chatted about their families and communities. Like his family near Lake Superior, her family lived near the Baltic Sea at

Simrishamn, so they shared experiences about boating.

When he expressed his interest in Viking ships, she offered to introduce him to Frans Gunnar Bengtson, author of the story *The Long Ships.*

"My family knows him," she explained, "and I'm sure he will be interested in your sailing the Great Lakes on a boat hauling iron ore. He advocates for the Jews, too, which generates mixed reactions in Sweden. Some of the German students at the University protested and even threatened him when he spoke at the University a few weeks ago."

Before long, Karl felt the German arrogance in Dr. Berghoff's class about German art. When Karl asked about the closing of the Bauhaus, one of the Germans berated him as a misinformed American. Dr. Berghoff also stated that the Americans evidently weren't aware of the Communist influence at the Bauhaus. "Now that those leaders have fled to America, they will give your country a taste of their radical beliefs."

Later in the term, the discussion related to a more comfortable topic for Karl—the influence of German art in supporting Luther's Reformation. From Durer and Cranach, the dialogue shifted to the role of the German goldsmiths who influenced Gutenberg in the development of his revolutionary movable type.

During an informal evening gathering at the home of Dr. Johansson, members of his class and their friends commended Karl for his impact on the department.

"Everywhere I turn in the department, your ideas and example seem to stir up discussion," said one student.

"That certainly affects Dr. Berghoff's study of German art," said another student, "especially among the German students in the class. Hope you can stand the guff," he added, using an American term.

"Dr. Berghoff doesn't exactly endorse your friendship with Inge, either," said another, as she looked to Inge for confirmation.

"I have to admit that my popularity doesn't rank high everywhere at the University," laughed Karl. "When I turned out to play some friendly soccer, I admitted that Americans don't know much about the game. But a few of the Germans and their aggressive Swedish friends offered a quick lesson. My black eye and a few other bruises are finally fading, but the animosity doesn't seem to fade."

As the conversation turned to personal reflections, others shared information about their families and communities—including Stockholm. When they heard about the locations of Karl's relatives, several offered information and help in connecting with his Swedish family.

With the gathering winding down, Inge volunteered: "I came alone, and so did Karl. So I think I should walk him home to ensure his safety."

"Courageous!" shouted another student, as the others cheered and clapped.

"See how American we are becoming," laughed Inge.

"I need all the help I can get," said Karl, "so I accept the offer—gladly," as he reached for Inge's hand. "See how American I am," he laughed.

On the way to the apartment, she squeezed his hand and said, "I've told my family about you, and they're interested in meeting an American artist. So I wonder if you'd be willing to go home with me to visit during our next holiday?"

"That would be great!" exclaimed Karl. "I'm curious about your family and what you told about your dad's business. Industrial equipment fascinates me."

"Strange for an artist," laughed Inge.

"Not if you saw some of my paintings of the steam engine and the propellers of the boats on the Great Lakes," said Karl.

"I'd like to," she said, "and so would my parents."

"I guess I'll have to get busy and paint what I remember...but where can I get the pressed-wood panels I'm used to?" laughed Karl.

"Maybe ships here use those panels for packing, too," said Inge.

"So let's haunt the harbor," suggested Karl.

"I'm game," answered Inge.

"Well, you do sound and act like an American!" said Karl. "Makes me feel at home."

At the door, she said, with a giggle, "You can release my hand now."

"Only for a hug in trade," said Karl.

"American custom again?" asked Inge, with another giggle.

"Yup," said Karl, as he wrapped his arms around her, and she hugged him in return.

When he started to kiss her, she announced: "Not on the first date. An American rule, I believe."

"How about the Swedish rule, then?" he asked.

"For that you would have a much longer wait," she declared. Then, looking up at him with her warm smile, she added, "You look so forlorn." So she kissed him quickly and turned to go to her apartment.

The next day, Karl left a short query for Kjell in the workshop toolbox: "I met the fascinating Inge Lindfelt. Any chance she has a German connection?"

Kjell's answer brought Karl great relief. "Inge and her family have no sympathy for the Germans. She's great! Don't let her get away from you!"

Karl had tinkered with the radio earlier to report in, but had little information of interest. He thanked Kjell for the quick approval of Inge, explaining he had enlisted her to help prowl the waterfront, partly to look for scrap wood panels for painting. Also, he told of plans to visit a Swedish factory that could be a target for German espionage. He relayed his hopes to head north to visit a forest products facility. Even that, he admitted, would be far from the Swedish iron mines and the German transportation line across Sweden to the port of Narvik in Norway. He noted his encounters with some German students and possibly some Swedish sympathizers of Germany. He said he'd keep an eye on them, but more likely someone not so obvious might surface as a threat to his role in intelligence work.

After a few weeks in a routine course related to the basics of architecture, Prof. Gustafsson talked privately with Karl.

"First," he said, "I'm very impressed by your drawings and the concepts and details in support of them, and I'd like to have you show them to the class and share information about them.

"Also, I got information from within our department—Miss Lindfelt, to be specific about the source—that you have had some association with Frank Lloyd Wright. I, for one, would like to hear more, and I'm sure your fellow students would as well."

Surprised, Karl cautioned: "My association with Mr. Wright was very limited, but I did get acquainted with several of his students at Taliesin in Wisconsin. I would be willing to share in a discussion, if we include give and take. I'm afraid I wouldn't be very effective as a lecturer."

"That sounds just what I'd like," said the professor. "I'll announce the topic for next Friday, if that suits you."

When Prof. Gustafsson and Karl entered the packed room, they were both surprised at the size of the crowd. "I guess you attracted an interested group," said Prof. Gustafsson with Swedish understatement.

"I hope I don't disappoint them," said Karl.

"Well, I primed some in our class with questions in case the discussion lags. But I doubt it," he added, with a smile of satisfaction.

Karl looked to the side to see Inge, and she smiled reassurance.

To open the 'forum', Karl explained he would be speaking in English although he did understand Swedish, but it was easier to use when explaining about his studies in the U.S. Then he said, "Before I started my studies of art history and architecture at the University of Wisconsin, I worked one summer at Frank Lloyd Wright's residence and school called Taliesin. That means 'brow of the hill,' I believe, and here's a drawing I just prepared from memory. It may lack accuracy, but it conveys the basic character of the place."

Karl's fellow students, impressed by Karl's drawing and by Taliesin, began clapping, and others joined in.

"What did you do there?" asked a student.

"The residents raise most of their own food, so I tilled the soil, along with about 25 other 'students.' I tuned up the truck and tractor, and I even applied my limited welding skills to repair equipment," explained Karl. "And I got the opportunity to prepare drawings like this for some of the many projects at Taliesin."

A person in the back raised his hand. "You referred to students. How were they trained?"

"Most already had college degrees, some with advanced degrees, and some were already teaching architecture. I was an exception, because I just volunteered in the summer before starting college.

"The learning process might relate to this session, with our exchange of ideas. I got advice about the handling of perspective, for example. In turn, I shared ideas about adding color to drawings. In fact, one of the drawings I prepared there was included in an exhibit of my paintings in the small town of Richland Center in Wisconsin."

"Did you meet Frank Lloyd Wright?" asked a young woman among the visitors.

"Most of the summer, he was away on projects," explained Karl. "The Johnson Wax building, if you know about that, had just been finished." Several nodded in recognition.

"Sorry to say that I haven't seen it yet, nor the 'Fallingwater' structure in Pennsylvania. But that had just been completed." More nods and smiles spread around the room.

"But, I repeat," laughed the woman who offered the question, "did you get to meet him?"

"Yes, but I really cut it close. Mr. Wright, as the others called him, returned the last day before I left for college. The others had a farewell lunch for me—we ate outside most of the summer—and Mr. Wright called me forward. He thanked me for my work, and he complimented me on my drawings. Then he presented me with a drawing he had produced when he was my age. Signed, framed and with a note from him. And that's carefully preserved at my parents' home in Wisconsin," smiled Karl.

"How would you compare him to our Mr. Asplund?" asked a student.

"First, I'm sorry about the recent death of Mr. Asplund, and sorry I didn't have a chance to meet him," said Karl. "Like the work of Mr. Wright, his architecture evolved from the formal to functional. But perhaps Mr. Wright started at a stage where Mr. Asplund's career ended. So Mr. Wright could experiment more, maybe because of the greater opportunities in America.

"As you may know, Mr. Wright often tries techniques and materials before they have been tested, such as the columns of the Johnson Wax building and the glass tubing in the roof. Unfortunately, because of his experiments, his buildings often leaked," laughed Karl.

Another woman in the class raised her hand. "How were you treated by those extraordinary students?"

"As I indicated, they respected me, included me in the group, and taught me. And they appreciated my welding when I helped with their sculpture," added Karl, with a slight smile.

"Now picture this," continued Karl, with a grin. "At the time of the exhibit of my art, about a dozen of them came riding into town, sitting on the back of a flatbed truck. The radio station welcomed the opportunity to interview them, so the art show got more publicity and attendance for the rest of the week."

"You said your art show was broadcast on the radio—how could art be shown on the radio?" asked a visitor.

"I wondered that myself," smiled Karl, "but the announcer talked with me about the art, asked about the paint sources—such as the iron ore and the dyes from the Indians—and got opinions from viewers. Amazingly, the broadcast generated great response and pulled in many more visitors."

A student from the Art History class asked about the drawing of Taliesin. "I noticed that your painting of Taliesin wasn't on canvas or cardboard. What is that?"

"Do we have time for another explanation?" Karl asked, as he looked at Prof. Gustafsson. He nodded yes, as did many others.

"Well, I should turn this over to my collaborator, Inge Lindfelt," said Karl, as he pointed toward her, and she smiled in embarrassment and shook her head "no."

Before he began explaining, Karl noticed the glare from Dr. Berghoff, but he proceeded without a hitch as he briefly thought of the growing personal conflict.

"This is a thin pressed-wood panel with a hard surface," he explained, as he showed the edges and front and back of the panel. "When I worked on a ship on the Great Lakes, panels like this—called Masonite—helped protect some of the cargo. When the panels got damaged, the crew discarded them. But I managed to salvage smaller sections for my 'canvas'. Because that's all I could afford," laughed Karl, and his audience laughed with him.

"Inge and I found almost the same thing in Malmö, but this is a Swedish product. As you can see, it works great, too."

Then Prof. Gustafsson announced, as he saw several hands go up: "One more question." So he called on a member of his class.

"How do you expect to use your architectural training in the future?"

"That's a frightening question," replied Karl, "because the way much of the world looks now, I'll be helping repair our war-damaged towns and cities for a long time to come."

After Karl's somber conclusion, the audience clapped and even cheered, and several came forward to thank him.

Impressed by Karl's responses in class, Prof. Gustafsson asked whether Karl might be willing to be the American representative in a forum involving a few selected student leaders from the university.

"The theme will be economics," said Prof. Gustafsson, "but that can include lots of topics, including the arts."

"I wonder if I really fit in that elite bunch," said Karl, when he heard about the five other participants. But the professor assured him that his American insights rather than his expertise would serve the purpose of the discussion.

Once again, he was surprised by the large turnout. But he was pleased to see many from the arts classes. Sitting at the front of the crowd, Inge again offered a reassuring smile. And so did Jenny Henriksson, from the art class.

After the others shared opinions about trends in capitalism, labor, taxation and the role of government in Sweden, the monitor called on Karl for his thoughts about how American attitudes related to the volatile conditions of Europe.

"Like Sweden, the United States wants to avoid involvement in the spreading war in Europe, with a large part of our population and our leadership determined to stay out of the conflict. And, also like here, we have an abundance of agricultural products to sell. Also, I know from personal experience on a ship on the Great Lakes, we have, like Sweden, lots of iron ore to sell.

"In another comparison to Sweden, the severe economic depression has paralyzed the United States in many ways. If you want a sense of the problem in America, read the new book called *Grapes of Wrath*. That's about desperate families moving from the middle of the country to California—a distance and challenge like moving from here to Lapland.

"Besides that, with the previous war well within memory, the people of United States are suffering from anxiety about the aggression of Germany.

"In fact, I recall that in political science classes at the University of Wisconsin, we scoffed at the ideas Hitler expressed in his *Mein Kampf*. Now his evolving predictions have stunned our nation!"

Sensing a pause, the monitor asked: "Do you think the United States will get actively involved?"

Karl responded cautiously: "Once again, like Sweden, we are selling goods related to the war, but ours go primarily to Britain. Shipments elsewhere probably would be blocked, you might say.

"As an emerging world power, the United States might be drawn in, like it or not," said Karl.

Then another member of the panel asked: "Doesn't the United States feel concern about the invaded Scandinavian countries, because of the Scandinavian immigration in America?"

"To a limited degree," explained Karl. "But remember, we have far more German than Scandinavian immigrants—about in the proportion the present Scandinavian population is to Germany's."

"Yes, I get the picture," responded the panelist. "We have 15 million people to Germany's 75 million."

Chapter 13: HOME AWAY FROM HOME

During a break at school, Karl enjoyed accompanying Inge on the train to her home in Helsingborg. She told about her family—father Tore, mother Hanna, younger sister Anja, and younger brother Jakob. "And our cat, Katrina."

She told more about her father's business that machined precision parts, including bearings, for a variety of equipment. Her mother, she explained, works for a state facility to help troubled teenage boys.

"Even in Sweden," asked a surprised Karl, "you have problems with behavior?"

"Oh yes," explained Inge, "the war increased the problem, with many young boys admiring the Nazis and acting like hoodlums. Of course, family problems and mental illness cause much of that behavior."

"I hope your family doesn't object to your inviting an American to visit," said Karl, "but this will show me of another side of Sweden."

"To say the least, they're all curious," said Inge. "I think my parents worry that we might become too serious, though they do admire Americans—especially an American with Swedish ancestry. They have mixed feelings about the British, and strong feelings against the Germans. Well, at least the Germans now in power."

After that comment, Karl asked, "Would it be possible and safe to go to Denmark so I could see for myself how the Germans are controlling that country?"

"Well, I as a neutral Swede and you an American, we can visit there, and shop and do other business there," explained Inge. "So let's count on taking the ferry there before we return to Lund. But I'll check with my parents first, in case they know of any concerns."

Inge's parents proved to be warm and friendly, as they welcomed Inge home with hugs and kisses. They shook hands with Karl and expressed their pleasure about his visit.

In their large home with a view of the Kattegat, Anja and Jakob bombarded Karl with questions, especially about sports in America.

"You look like a sports star," said Jakob.

"Like Swedish sports stars I've seen," said Anja.

"But not soccer," laughed Karl, "because some of the students at Lund really roughed me up because I didn't know what I was doing. But if we try football, they might suffer some bruises."

"How about hockey?" asked Jakob. "We have skilled players in Sweden."

"In Wisconsin too," smiled Karl.

"Sweden has champion skiers, too," said Anja. "But I suppose Wisconsin does, too."

Inge noticed that Karl didn't respond quickly. As he answered with a soft voice, she noticed tears in his eyes.

So she changed the subject to art, and all expressed curiosity about his learning from an Indian friend.

"And he doesn't use canvas to paint on," Inge explained, and her dad wondered about what he used. "You should have seen us, down at the port in Malmö, scrounging for discarded panels to salvage for his 'canvas'. You'd be surprised, Dad, how quickly Karl learned his way around the dock."

"I hope you were careful," said Hanna, "a port, even in Sweden, can be a rough place."

"I think he shows that he fits there, so no one bothered us," said Inge.

"Some of the seamen sure enjoyed looking at Inge," said Karl, "and I don't blame them. Your daughter is an appealing person, more than just to look at."

Anja and Jacob giggled as Inge blushed. "That's his American style," explained Inge, "and I'm starting to get used to it."

"I like the activity of the port, and it sounds like you do too," said Tore. "But Wisconsin is in the middle of America, isn't it?"

"Yes," said Karl, "but we have the Great Lakes, and I lived near Lake Superior and worked on a ship there."

"So you're a sailor from Wisconsin," confirmed Hanna, with some concern in her voice.

"I worked there for a year to earn money so I could go to the University of Wisconsin," explained Karl. "Fortunately, my dad works as a marine architect at the Port of Duluth, so he helped me get the job. I sailed until the lakes froze, then worked in the port the rest of the time."

"So you're one of those sailors who likes to look at pretty girls," giggled Anja.

"Oh, yes," smiled Karl, "if I was on the bow of a ship and saw a cute girl like you, I would certainly stare. And I'd try to get a date with you."

"No you won't," laughed Inge, "I found you first."

Conversation during meals and other times in the holiday explored more about the war and the attitudes in the United States and Sweden.

"I'm curious about the Germans," said Karl. "Inge said we might be able to visit Denmark, even though the Germans occupy the country. But she said we should check with you to be sure it would be okay."

Tore pondered the question, and Hanna looked concerned. Finally, he said, "A Swede and an American should be able to visit there without problem, but you'd have to avoid any confrontation or exploring beyond the retail area."

"Dad, Karl told me he has painted scenes of machinery, such as the steam engine of his ship," said Inge the next day. "And he's curious about what your factory makes. I think he sees a painting of gears and bearings in his mind already, so I wonder if you could take him—us—on a tour. I like seeing all those machines, too."

"As you can imagine," said Tore, "security is extremely tight now, because of the importance of our product and the proximity to the Germans in Denmark. And the British and Russians make us nervous, too.

"So I'll have to get authorization through the state security system. I hope you don't mind if I provide your name, Karl, to get clearance."

"That sure makes sense," said Karl, "and feel free to provide my name and background as needed."

"I'll let you know, Inge—and Karl," said Tore. "I'd sure enjoy showing off our plant and products."

"Interested in a walking tour of our port of Helsingborg?" asked Inge. "We have lots of light yet this evening."

"Sounds great to me!" said Karl.

"May we come along?" asked Anja.

"I'm not sure," laughed Inge, "Karl might ask you out on a date. You know how romantic these American men are."

"I vote yes, for Anja and Jakob," smiled Karl.

"Then I do also," said Inge.

Tore and Hanna smiled as they watched the foursome heading out for their evening stroll. "I sure enjoy having Karl here, and I think you do, too," said Hanna. "He seems like you with his interests. And Anja and Jakob sure take to him."

"You can add Inge to that," said Tore, "because she glows in his presence."

"As he does with her," added Hanna.

Along the way, Anja and Jakob pointed out the sights of the community. Whenever they ran into a friend or neighbor, they quickly introduced their American visitor.

"You have a lovely neighborhood and a beautiful view of the harbor and ocean," said Karl. "Makes me feel right at home, because it reminds me of looking out at Lake Superior."

A little later, Jakob nudged Anja and giggled, "Look at them, holding hands."

"I heard that," laughed Karl. "In America, we learned to be chivalrous, so when I sensed Inge getting chilly, I felt obligated to warm her hand."

"Oh, I think you Americans make up excuses," said Anja. So Karl reached over and held her hand, too.

"Will you kiss her, like we saw in the American movie?" asked Jacob, with a grin.

"What movie was that?" asked Karl, in anticipation of a torrid love scene.

"I think it was Andy Hardy," said Jacob.

"And Judy Garland," added Anja.

"Well, I have to admit that your sister sure is appealing, but she might not find an American so appealing," said Karl. "But maybe the two of you could tell her it would be all right for me to kiss her. After all, we are good friends. And isn't that what friends are for?"

"You Americans sure can come up with excuses," laughed Inge. "And you two can't vote on it, because I'll decide for myself."

At home, they all reported in.

"We had a great walk, with beautiful scenery, met many friendly people, and had fun chatting," said Karl. "I learned that Jakob and Anja like to tease."

"We're just learning the American way," laughed Anja.

"Well, come on in the kitchen and warm up with some hot chocolate," said Hanna. "I believe that's American, too."

"We learned that an American man helps keep a woman warm by holding her hand," said Anja, as Hanna and Tore smiled at each other.

"Well, he held your hand, too," said Jakob. "So he's chivalrous—I think that's the word he used."

Later, as Inge and Karl sat in the porch swing and watched the sun go down, Karl, with his arm around her, asked why she was so quiet during the walk.

"I was just enjoying being with you, and our family," she said.

After a pause, she continued, quietly: "I was concerned about you. I saw the sadness in your face and the tears in your eyes when Anja asked about skiing. If you want to talk about it, I'll listen," she said as she snuggled against him.

"I do feel deep sadness...I lost...I lost my best friend, my lover, because she was killed in an accident on the way...on the way to a skiing competition," he said softly.

"I'm so sorry," she responded, as she felt his tears against her cheek.

"Thanks," he murmured. "I am truly thankful to have you as a friend...someone with qualities equal to hers. At the time of her death, I felt life wasn't worth living. Now I know it is," he said, as he placed his hand gently on her cheek. He turned her face toward him and kissed her softly.

She responded by hugging him tightly and kissing him firmly.

"I'm honored that you've included me in your life," she whispered.

Inge stayed up to talk with her parents after the others went to bed.

"Good news!" said Tore. "Karl and the rest of you are authorized to visit the factory. And the Swedish security office approved that in record time."

"That should be interesting, and I look forward to Karl's response," said Inge.

"I wanted to mention to you a sad reaction he showed earlier, when Anja asked about skiing," she added.

"I noticed that her question seemed to trigger a look of sorrow on his face and in his posture," said Hanna. "Do you know why?"

"I asked him this evening about that," said Inge, "and he had considerable difficulty expressing his feelings."

"That does seem unusual," said Tore, "after we talked about the openness of Americans."

"Pardon me if I shed some tears," said Inge, "but I learned that he lost his best friend…actually, his lover, he said…when she was killed in a bus accident on the way to a skiing competition."

"How tragic!" said Hanna, as Tore reached out to touch Inge and Hanna. "I hope our family can provide some solace…but I wonder whether our happiness might add to his sadness."

"No, he thanked me for being a friend at a time he had thought life was not worth living," said Inge. "And I think our family can be important to him, too."

"We hope so," said Tore, "because already he seems to fit in so well with our family."

"I enjoy the way he jokes around with Anja and Jakob," said Hanna, "and he's so pleasant and interesting to be with.

"I sense that your feelings are already much deeper," added Hanna. "I wouldn't want you to suffer sadness if he is just turning to you as a replacement lover."

"From the time we first met—when we were both welding in the school shop," she laughed, and Tore and Hanna also laughed about the unusual situation, "we enjoyed talking and being together.

"He hasn't indicated that I'm like her in appearance or personality or even mentioned her name, so I hope he likes me for me. And, no, I don't intend to become his lover. But I do think I already love him."

"You can count on us to offer support to both of you," said Hanna. "And I think we already love him, too."

During the tour of the Lindfelt plant, Karl admired the skilled draftsmen as they designed components ordered by the customers. Then he absorbed impressions of the machines producing parts like those in the drawings. He also scoped the facility and how it might be damaged by potential sabotage, so he could report to the Swedish intelligence some possible protective measures.

That night, after a stimulating mealtime discussion of the tour, Karl borrowed some sketching paper and colored pencils from Inge.

In the morning, he unveiled an impression of the machining of a part.

"How did you get that smoky effect, so other lines would stand out?" asked Anja. "I sure like it!"

Karl explained his approach of rubbing in subtle colors to contrast the hardness of the machine and the sense of movement from the strips of metal being removed as a part was created.

"I found it fascinating, a scene similar to the aura of welding," said Karl.

Inge hugged him, and exclaimed, "That depicts a marvelous feeling and sense of creation."

"I produced this in appreciation for your charming family and your gracious hospitality," said Karl, as he handed the drawing to Hanna.

"How can you part with that, when it shows you so much!" said Hanna. "We thank you deeply."

"Art sure looks different to me now," said Jakob. "This seems so rugged, yet pretty."

Tore spoke quietly: "You've captured my life, my work. I never realized the beauty of it before."

"So many artists have inspired me," explained Karl, during a discussion of art later during a gathering of the family, relatives and friends of the Lindfelts.

"Well," commented Tore, "you do seem like a refreshing contrast to the typical artists we hear about."

"I'd say that about your daughter, too," as Karl turned to smile at Inge and touch her hand. "I sensed she was special when I saw her as she lifted her welding mask."

"Well, then, besides Inge, what artists do you admire and emulate?" asked a friend of the family.

"Maybe I shouldn't admit this because of conditions in Europe right now," explained Karl, "but I like and learn from the drawings and paintings of Lyonel Feininger. But he is an American, though a German American.

"I get encouragement from the practicality of much of his art. I appreciate his cartoons as well as his geometric forms."

"How about a Swedish artist?" asked Jacob.

"Prins Eugen surprises me most," said Karl. "I guess in America, we don't expect royalty to be artists, but I do admire his landscapes."

"I think in Sweden, too, we don't expect royalty to be artists, but his art is popular and appreciated here, too," said Inge.

"We hope to get a chance to meet with the artists who have banded together in an art community in Halmstad," continued Inge. "Maybe on the way to Gothenburg some day, if we can arrange it."

"I'd welcome that!" said Karl. "Amazing to have that group of artists from one community, including three from one family. From the magazine you showed me, I particularly like the paintings by Erik Olson. One of his landscapes reminds me of paintings by Grant Wood of Iowa, not far from Wisconsin."

"Oh, yes," said Inge, "Grant Wood got lots of attention at the Art Academy in Minneapolis. We learned that his success occurred when he decided to return to paint what he knew—in Iowa, instead of Europe.

"By the way, Halmstad displays a Carl Milles sculpture in its city center," said Inge, "and you might find that interesting, too."

"Great! Because of all the Swedish artists, Milles ranks as my most familiar," said Karl, "because America includes much his sculpture.

"In some ways, his background matches mine, in contrast to Prins Eugen, because Milles was a craftsman with metal before he advanced in art.

"And I've admired his sculpture of an Indian in the city hall of St. Paul, in Minnesota. Not far from my home."

"I heard about it, but didn't see it myself," said Inge. "But that relates to your mentioning how Indians made dyes for their colors."

"As I told Inge earlier, a high school friend was from the Ojibway tribe in our area, and I learned much about art and life from him.

"That reminds me of another Swedish artist, who lives in America," said Karl. "Carl Oscar Borg also is a pragmatist, like what I think I am. And he prefers painting scenes of the Indians of southwestern United States."

"Your art sounds better all the time," said Jakob.

"Here's part of Mr. Borg's life you might especially like, Jakob," explained Karl. "He painted many scenes for the backgrounds of movies, including sailing ships in one movie about pirates."

"Do you know of other Swedish artists?" asked a young woman cousin of Inge.

"Anders Zorn painted charming scenes of rural Sweden, and Swedish women," said Karl. "His portraits of several leaders, including American presidents, were powerful. Wish I could do that!"

"You will!" said Inge, bursting with pride.

"Have you heard of our Carl Larsson?" asked a matron from the neighborhood.

"Oh, what fun he can evoke with his family and home and farm," said Karl. "Once again, I admire his skill and his pragmatic style. And his sense of humor.

"But I understand that he died just a few years ago. I regret missing a chance to meet him and learning from him," said Karl.

"His reputation really grew when color printing improved, so more people could see his drawings and paintings," explained Karl. "He reminds me of our American artist, Norman Rockwell, and his charming illustrations for our magazines."

"Those are fun, and insightful," said Inge. "I saw his covers of the *Saturday Evening Post* when I studied in Minneapolis. They make you smile in empathy and appreciation."

With that shift in the conversation, Inge finally got a chance to talk about her interests and intentions related to art.

"We know you're a welder. What else?" asked her uncle.

"Even in Sweden, which we consider to be progressive, women face difficulties when they choose a career other than teaching or nursing," said Inge. "Perhaps illustrating for magazines will provide an opportunity for me."

"Seems like your dad could find a place for you in the growing field of industrial design," said her aunt.

"Good possibility," said Tore.

"And speaking of industrial design," said Tore, "before we part ways tonight, I want to show you a drawing Karl created for us…that seems to symbolize the essence of our life."

When he held up Karl's drawing of the machinist at the plant, several exclaimed their approval, and a few even clapped. Anja and Jakob came over to hug Karl from behind, while Inge squeezed his hand.

Chapter 14: VENTURE TO DENMARK

On the final day of their holiday, Karl and Inge boarded the ferry to go to Denmark.

"Will the ghost of Hamlet greet us when we land in Elsinore?" asked Karl. "Sometimes I mutter to myself like he did."

"The Danes call the town Helsingör, and a lot of them are probably muttering to themselves about the current changes in their life," said Inge.

"Don't know how you did it, but getting a Nimbus motorcycle and sidecar takes a lot of influence," said Inge, surprised by the special treatment in Denmark, and wondering whether Karl's stay in Sweden included more than study at Lund.

"I cut a deal in advance, because the Germans want to impress us Americans," said Karl. "Charles Lindbergh, the famous Swedish-American flyer, sure got special treatment, with the hope by the Germans that he would share his impressions about the Luftwaffe."

"Did he?" asked Inge.

"He really put a scare into our country when he reported about the German advancements in aviation," explained Karl. "He put a scare into our president, too, because he has been trying to calm the American people…while secretly supporting Britain."

"Well," said Inge, "the sun is out, so this should be a great day for our short tour!"

"We should even get a look at the North Sea by driving along the shore, maybe have a picnic at a quiet and comfortable spot," said Karl, at the same time as he was thinking about his assignment to watch for any sign of German buildup along the western side of Denmark.

When they returned, curiosity prevailed during dinner, as all of Inge's family asked questions.

Jakob led off, grinning, "Did you tangle with any Germans today?"

Hanna chided him, as Karl responded, also with a grin, "I had to beat up on a couple of German rowdies who started to flirt with Inge."

"You can see that he likes to create stories as well as art," laughed Inge. "Actually, we had a great time. The German soldiers assumed Karl was just a big and tall Swede, but then they got interested when they learned he is from America. They even asked about some cities where they had relatives in America.

"Then they seemed to realize why their commander had allowed our use of the motorcycle— to curry favor with an American."

"I had an interesting time talking with them," said Karl, "considering our language difficulties."

"The Danes seem to be functioning well, under the circumstances," said Inge, "but we worried that some Dane might seek a favor from us and cause a dangerous situation."

"Yes, we could sense a prevailing undercurrent of tension," agreed Karl.

"Strangely, we ran into a worse problem back in Sweden, on the waterfront," said Inge, as her family tensed. "Two big merchant seamen started to grab me. You should have seen the action then, Jakob. It was fast!"

"What happened?" asked an eager Jakob, as the others also waited alertly for her explanation.

"Well, I don't really know," said Inge, as the others looked disappointed.

"After some quick slashes by Karl, the other two were on the ground groaning," said Inge.

"So you're a fighter as well as an artist," said an admiring Anja.

"Usually I just run," laughed Karl, as he tried to play down the situation, "but this time I certainly had to defend Inge."

"By the speed of your response, you must have had some good training," said Tore, as he continued to wonder if Karl was more than just a student.

"I thank my Indian friend, because he helped me sharpen my defensive skills," said Karl, to cover up his Commando training. "After this incident, I sure do appreciate the times we challenged each other."

"I knew it!" said Jakob, "because you seem to move agilely, like an Indian."

"For that," said Karl, "I'll get you a copy of *The Last of the Mohicans*. And you'll find the paintings of Indians by N.C. Wyeth to be rewarding to look at."

"I've heard of him, along with other American artists like him," said Inge. "Maybe I'll be able to illustrate books like that some day."

Inge and Karl waved at her saddened family as the train departed for Lund.

"I feel so comfortable with your family," said Karl, "and I can't thank you enough for inviting me. They—and you—have helped me during a difficult time."

"I enjoyed so much being with you," she said as she put her head on his shoulder. "And I learned so much, as the others did, about such a wide range of art. And thanks for defending me so gallantly and skillfully. Now I appreciate Indians more than ever before," she laughed.

"Going back to school will be a letdown after such a wonderful holiday," said Karl, "but you will bring continual joy for me."

"And you for me," she said.

That night, Karl activated the radio and reported what he had learned during the holiday. He stressed the importance of Tore's plant, with its capability for precision machining and other production. He said he had learned that much of the output went to the Volvo plant in Gothenburg.

Karl suggested that the Swedish intelligence organization might increase its presence at the port of Helsingborg. Maybe some ongoing military maneuvers there could coincidently help protect that vital facility.

He thanked Kjell for arranging for the use of the motorcycle in Denmark, and it seemed credible that the Germans would make allowances for an American visitor. Once, anyway.

The visit there may have produced some valuable clues about secret German activity on the west coast of Denmark. In friendly conversation about America, some Germans casually mentioned the start of construction of a small airfield and a special concrete bunker there.

The soldiers had bragged that the bunker would house some new electronic equipment that might even dazzle Americans. Probing for more information seemed too risky. But the British in particular might want to analyze what the equipment could be and what it might mean to them.

Next, he said he would watch for German counterparts who might be watching him.

Also, Karl mentioned interest in visiting a paper mill in northern Sweden as part of his study of pulp as a new art "canvas." Could be a good excuse to survey the shipping in the area.

Back in Helsingborg, Tore first shared with Hanna his concerns about Karl's unusual situation. He explained that he worried about any possibility of a threat to the plant…and any other possible threats to Helsingborg.

"Maybe Karl could even be a German spy," Tore cautiously confided to Hanna. "His good fortune in getting the use of the motorcycle seems suspicious. And so does his sudden skill in defending Inge."

"But he's such a fine person, and he's so amazingly knowledgeable about art and architecture…and he enchanted our family and friends," said Hanna, with a tinge of sadness.

"That makes me worry about Inge," said Hanna, "because she seems so fond of Karl. She would be heartbroken if he's not genuine."

"I know," said Tore, "and that's another reason I want to investigate right away. I'm going to reach as high as I can in our national security organization, both to warn them and to protect our family and our plant."

"I hope you succeed, but I'll be on edge waiting and wondering," said Hanna. "I'll try not to give an indication to Anja and Jakob, and certainly not to Inge."

Tension increased in Kjell Seastrand's Swedish intelligence organization, as Tore pressed for answers. The concern extended to Col. Haaken Hansen, as he monitored the American intelligence activity throughout Scandinavia.

Finally, Kjell and Haaken agreed that they needed quell Tore's concern about Karl. Their investigations confirmed that Tore's allegiance to Sweden was beyond reproach. And they concluded that he would be completely trustworthy with secret information.

When Kjell asked to meet with Tore on behalf of Swedish intelligence, Tore insisted that Hanna participate, because she already knew of his concern.

So, the Lindfelts hosted Kjell and Haaken in what appeared to be a casual lunch at their home. Tension continued, though, as Kjell and Haaken displayed their credentials, outlined their knowledge of the Lindfelt family and associates, and expressed their concern for the safety of the plant.

"We're concerned for our daughter, Inge," said an anguished Hanna, fearing the worst outcome.

Slowly and systematically, Kjell and Haaken revealed Karl's role in the joint intelligence activity.

At first, Tore was upset that the security operation had invaded their family, but Hanna sank back in relief that her fearful assumptions had dissolved.

"I admit," said Haaken, "that Karl's potentially dangerous role could also jeopardize your family. But bear in mind, the spreading war puts him at great personal risk.

"To ease your worries for Inge, let me assure you that Karl's a brilliant, talented and honorable person," said Haaken. "Unfortunately, your daughter's commitment to him could lead to sorrow because of the risks he might face."

"I am so greatly relieved," said Hanna. "We are personally fond of Karl, and I'm sure Inge has already committed herself to him."

"From reading between the lines in what I hear from Karl," said Haaken, "I believe he is fully committed to Inge as well."

"Thanks for putting our minds at ease," said Tore. "But how do we proceed now?"

"Please don't reveal this information to anyone, including Inge," said Haaken. "Karl's role can be so important to all who oppose the Nazis, even to the security of Sweden."

"Already he has urged protection of your plant," said Kjell, "and you soon will notice certain military maneuvers near your plant. That process will be part of the security."

Chapter 15: BACK TO THE CLASSROOM

In Karl's classes, which were more like forums, he enjoyed the mix of lectures, the reports from the students, and the discussions of assignments.

Art Sleuths

Except the class about German art, which became more and more a confrontation between him and Prof. Lindhof. The German students joined in the fray, verbally attacking Karl because he questioned the purpose of the current German art. Then Inge suffered verbal abuse from Prof. Lindhof and the two Germans when she tried to turn the disagreements into positive dialogue.

"We heard about your interest in runic letters," scoffed one of the Germans. "Our leaders like them too. And the runic letters 'SS' indicate our military 'storm squad' with 'special scope' in Germany now."

"I know," said Karl, "a threatening application of ancient letter forms."

Slowly the other students rallied in support of Karl. Jenny Henriksson, another articulate and personable woman in the class, added her vigorous resistance to the professor.

There was no more time to pursue the topic because the class ended, although the German students scowled as they left the room.

After class, Jenny made a point to talk with Karl and Inge, and from time to time she joined them in conversations over coffee and sometimes at lunch.

Jenny explained that she found Karl's position as an American at a Swedish university to be intriguing, and she encouraged Karl to share his feelings and opinions.

"I'm getting jealous," laughed Inge later, after one conversation among the three of them, when Jenny continued to inquire about Karl's life at the University of Wisconsin. "Well, she is attractive…and certainly attentive."

Karl answered with a hug.

After one class, Jenny explained that she had heard the German students talking about military training at American universities. "Is that true? And were you involved?" she asked.

Karl laughed about her question, as he answered, "Yup, we made money by going to lectures and marching once in a while, so that helped me pay my bills at the university. But, unlike what I've heard about a lot of young Germans, most American students don't take it very seriously."

Inge listened with interest—also when Jenny asked if Karl had visited other countries in Europe.

"Only England," said Karl. "And Denmark a short time ago."

"I suppose you stopped in England on the way to Sweden," said Jenny.

"Actually, I attended Cambridge there," said Karl.

"Impressive!" said Jenny.

Then Karl put his index finger on his closed lips: "Be like the Swedish tiger," he said, "just as the poster reminds you Swedes to be silent...so you don't give away secrets to foreigners.

"But that applies to us, not you. You're the foreigner," laughed Jenny, "so you don't have to be silent."

That night, after Karl thought about Jenny's curiosity, he began to wonder about her motives: *With her looks and brains and friendliness, she might fit the profile of a sophisticated German spy. She certainly could cause a person to relax and share information.*

In a radio exchange with Haaken, he described the situation. Haaken commended Karl for being alert to the subtle questioning. "I'll get back to you after I confer with Kjell."

When Haaken radioed back, he reported, "She sounds slick…and suspicious, so we want to test her. If she does work for the Nazis, we may be able to use her for our purposes in the future. We suggest you plan another visit to Denmark with Inge, with the excuse that an American newspaper would like an impression about life there now. Share that with Jenny only, and we'll have the Danish underground check to see if she leaks it to Nazi leaders there."

In Copenhagen, Karl and Inge went first to the museum displaying the sculpture of Bertel Thorvaldsen. They agreed that his work showed remarkable skill, but concluded that it seemed like a copy from the past.

"Maybe August Strindberg criticized that shallowness when he wrote about Thorvaldsen," said Inge.

"Let's watch for a chance to catch a Strindberg play at the University or somewhere else," suggested Karl. "Knowing more about Strindberg could add to my understanding of Sweden—as well as learning more about his painting and photography."

"Besides," said Inge, "his sharp tongue about life, even his anti-Semitism, could fit particularly well with the challenges we face right now."

In contrast, they reflected about the creative storytelling and paper-cutting of Hans Christian Andersen as they viewed an exhibit related to his life.

They noted his successful but often sad life. And they read that a previous war involving

Denmark caused him a loss of friends and a bout of depression.

"Ironically," Karl shared with Inge, "in that war, Denmark lost Schleswig and Holstein. Now, a German battleship with that name triggered this war by firing on a Polish military outpost."

As in the previous visit to Denmark, German soldiers looked for an opportunity to brag to an American.

When they learned of Karl and Inge's interest in art, one officer explained how Germany is helping Denmark in a special way. Many Danes are being employed to excavate the burial mound of King Gorm. "We share that heritage, too," said the officer. "And we're helping Danes in the present by paying them to explore their past."

In the Tivoli Gardens, an attendant explained that the amusement park had not been shut down since it opened about a century ago, and even war couldn't close it.

A Danish patron took the opportunity to whisper information to them. He told about the rumors related to the new German fortification for important secret activity on the west coast.

Though the German soldiers monitored the activities of Karl and Inge, they didn't interfere with the "neutrals" on a holiday. But when Karl and Inge approached the ferry to return home, German guards insisted on seeing Karl's notebook. They smiled in surprise and appreciation as they looked at his sketches of Thorvaldsen's sculpture, so they paid little attention to Karl's accompanying notes.

On the ferry back to Malmö, Inge snuggled against Karl, but he sensed her tenseness.

"Are you upset about today?" asked Karl. "You don't feel relaxed."

"Just thinking...about you," she said softly.

"Hmmm, something you want to share?" he asked.

"You cause me to reflect and wonder about your interesting...sometimes contradictory qualities. In Sweden, we tend to seek sameness...don't rock the boat, as you Americans might say. But you seem destined to rock the boat. But you also seem sensitive and concerned about others, as I feel we are in Sweden. And your concern for me shows in so many ways...which I cherish," she added, with a warm smile.

"I suppose...," he responded, with a pause. "I suppose I'm a throwback to the Vikings.

"And I'm so pleased and blessed to have you as my companion," he added, "with your special qualities. Actually, I think you are part American, too," he laughed, "with your initiative."

As she settled back with his arm around her, she declared: "Now I feel content and secure."

"Me too," he said, and kissed her on her forehead.

That night, Karl got a message from Haaken: "We think your Jenny Henriksson might be a German spy, because we learned that the Germans knew you were coming and had arranged to keep an eye on you. They also knew you were gathering information for an American newspaper. Now, to live up to your charade, we think you should actually write a story with your impressions and send it off to an American newspaper. We'll help make the arrangements. It looks like we've found a pipeline to the Germans. Good work!"

Chapter 16: RESEARCH OPPORTUNITY

Karl surprised Professor Johansson when he announced that he would be going on an interesting research project. He explained that he had arranged to take a trip north to study the pulp and paper process, and he planned to connect that with the history of art materials.

"That sounds like the research project by another Carl—by the name of Linnaeus!" exclaimed the professor, with a grin of approval.

"Well," explained Karl, "I did learn that he studied some plants for use in papermaking, so I suppose I can claim a minor connection to his major research."

Then he explained that the big forest products company Dolman had agreed to host him for a tour of the mills, the forests and, of special importance, a chance to visit the company's research facilities.

A stunned Inge listened with intense interest, and Jenny also showed great curiosity.

"This is quite a coup!" observed Jenny. "How in the world did you accomplish that?"

Karl explained that he needed to conduct unique research for his doctor's degree, so he pursued his interest in pulp and wood-based paper as it might relate to the future of design.

"As you may know, Carl Larsson's career in art benefited from improvements in printing, and much of his good fortune related to better printing paper.

"The company likes the link of paper to the art program here," continued Karl, "and the Dolman leaders certainly noted my connection to America. So they may visualize future opportunities for marketing in America.

"Good thing I'm familiar with the paper production in Wisconsin," said Karl. "At least I've visited a pulp and paper mill there to get acquainted with the process. That's when I saw the importance of art in relation to mass production of paper and printing.

"Of course, I don't know how Dolman might expect to market in America, with Germany controlling Swedish exports. Maybe the leaders see hope for joint investments with American companies."

Even Dr. Lindhof joined in with the enthusiasm of the rest of the faculty.

"I must commend you for creative thinking, Karl," he said. "This should bring great credit to our department and the university. Your study could produce some valuable change, especially, as you noted, in the field of publishing."

Inge's controlled excitement broke free when she and Karl shared lunch. "Marvelous!" she exclaimed. "Your endeavor exceeds any project the art department has had for years! I can hardly wait to learn what you learn," she said enthusiastically.

"My research venture might include another aspect of travel," he announced.

"Oh, no! I hope you don't plan to return to America," she said with sadness. "I don't want to part from you!"

"No, just the opposite," he said. "I'd like you to go north with me and share in the research project because I think it would benefit your studies."

She was quiet for several seconds. "Did I hear you say you want me to go along with you?"

"That's what I said," he answered.

"Let me think it over...for a few seconds," she said, with a big smile. "Okay, I've decided...and the answer is...that sounds wonderful!"

"Well, it may not be so wonderful, considering we'll be traveling to the mill on a tugboat. And I don't know what the accommodations might be in a mill town. And venturing into the forest might be rough going, too."

"I can hardly wait for that rough living and rough going...as long as I'm with you," she declared.

Chapter 17: REVELATION

"Something wrong?" she asked, as she noticed his seriousness, in spite of his promise of an interesting shared adventure.

"I need to explain a concern I have before we start this research trip," he said, again with a serious tone that caused her to wonder about a possible problem for their relationship.

"Let's take a walk so we can talk outside without being overheard," he said, as her anxiety increased.

"I lead a double life," he announced. Anxiously, she worried that he might be married...or what could it be?

"Besides being a student...who's in love with you...I have another life," he said, as he tried to ease into his explanation.

"I'm afraid to hear, you sound so mysterious and ominous," she said. "Please, just tell me."

"Okay," he said, cautiously, "I'm an agent serving the American and Swedish intelligence organizations...and as I just said, I love you and don't want to lose you!"

Stunned, she let go of his hand and started to cry. "I wish you had told me earlier, not keep that information from me...while I was falling in love with you. Now I don't know what to think!"

"My leaders in the intelligence agencies wanted me to continue keeping this from you," he explained. "I'm sorry about how this might affect us, but I decided that we shouldn't go on this trip together unless you knew about my whole life. Until now, I—and the agencies—have tried to protect you from involvement and risk. But, that might no longer be possible."

In a state of shock and crying softly, she said, "Now I need time to absorb this news and think about how it might affect my life...our life."

"I understand...and agree," he said, "but I don't want to lose you...and yet I can't avoid my responsibility to the intelligence agencies. Unfortunately, you would be drawn more and more into the intelligence activity by continued association with me.

"But, remember, my role for these agencies is honorable and important...just as you are so very important to me," he continued. "I lost one wonderful love in my life, and now I don't want to lose another."

"I know...and I love you so much," said Inge, "but I need to consider this new dimension of your life."

The next day, Inge declared, in a lilting voice, "I believe I'm ready for your dual life, though I may still have to ease into full acceptance."

"I'm truly thankful," said Karl, "that you accepted this news so quickly, after your initial shock."

"I called my parents to tell them about some of my concerns with our relationship. But they read between the lines," she said, "and they revealed that they had been worried earlier about some unusual aspects of your life. Eventually, the Swedish intelligence leader, Kjell Seastrand, explained to them your important work...and your outstanding ability and character. So they passed that along to me. And alerted Kjell.

"Later, Kjell called to reassure me, and to caution me about secrecy. Of course, I didn't have to be reminded of your outstanding ability and character. But he didn't mention your romantic nature," she added with a smile and hug.

"What a relief!" said Karl. "I was ready to abandon the trip if you wouldn't go along."

"And abandon me! No you don't," she laughed.

On the relaxing train ride north, they talked about both parts of Karl's research—the study of the potential impact of the paper industry in the field of art, and the gathering of information about the use of the transportation system in northern Sweden by the Germans.

"As you no doubt guessed by now," said Karl, "this project benefited from a lot of pressure by Kjell Seastrand. So, while we talk about art on one hand, we all know that the other hand deals with espionage."

He explained that "we'll get off at Bråviken to switch to a tugboat pulling a barge-load of equipment and material for the mill, which means we'll have a long boat ride ahead of us.

"But that will give us a taste of the Göta Canal, and a link to one of my heroes, John Ericsson. He worked on the Canal while still a teenager, and he later created the *Monitor* ironclad that was so important to the Union forces in our Civil War.

"We'll go by way of the Matala Strom, and the mill town there serves as a history of Sweden in a nutshell," said Karl, "including battles for control of Sweden, the development of manufacturing such as textiles, and refining agricultural products such as sugar."

"Thanks for the lecture about my country," laughed Inge.

"Anytime," smiled Karl, "even if I have to make up history on the spot.

"Beware, the start at the Baltic probably won't be smooth," warned Karl. "Hope you don't get seasick."

"No way," she countered, "after all the sailing our family has done."

"Now, I suggest we try to get some sleep, as best we can," said Karl, as he also thought of the pleasure of nestling with Inge, "because we will board the tugboat after a short meeting with some Dolman officials."

"Won't we be in great form for a business meeting," laughed Inge, "gritty and in our work clothes...and nothing more formal in my suitcase."

"They know we're dressed for the mill and forest," said Karl. "Besides, you look beautiful even in work clothes."

"That deserves a kiss," smiled Inge, as she snuggled against Karl.

The Dolman "business meeting" took place on the dock, before the tugboat set sail. Karl, with input from Inge, talked about changes in the printing industry, and he reported about the trends in Wisconsin about the making and marketing of pulp and paper. The Dolman officials told of the special grades of pulp produced in Sweden, and Karl explained that he had heard of the need for that kind of pulp to be mixed in with American pulp for higher-grade paper.

After handshakes and wishes for a safe journey by the officials, Karl and Inge joined Olav Olesson, the captain of the tug.

As the tug headed from the Baltic Sea into the river, big and friendly Olav explained that he might need help, particularly as a lookout for any obstructions that might have drifted into their route.

"That will add some challenge during our journey," smiled Inge.

Karl explained to Inge that they would also note the nature and amount of German shipping they might see. "We're trying to gather that information, without knowing exactly what to do with it, considering Sweden's neutrality. The data might be fed to the Norwegian resistance, which does carry out steady sabotage of German transportation across northern Sweden.

Hours later, the tired "watchers" welcomed the sight of the port. And they welcomed the hope for sleep.

Olav explained that town had no hotel, so Karl and Inge would stay at his place. When they arrived there, after docking the boat, his wife Helga welcomed them warmly...and with an invitation to an appetizing supper.

She chided Olav for the little food he had offered on the tug, but Karl and Inge explained that the meals he provided were adequate and tasty, even if they were simple. "Good coffee, too!" said Karl.

"And we enjoyed being with Olav," said Inge, as Olav looked embarrassed.

Later, Inge mentioned to Karl that Helga seemed concerned about the sleeping arrangements. "They only have two bedrooms, so she suggested that perhaps you and Olav could sleep together, and I could sleep with her."

"Well, I might as well shock you again," said Karl. "I think we could sleep together in the second bedroom."

Karl smiled at Inge's silence, and he added: "After we're married."

"Did you just propose?" smiled Inge.

"Yup, and Olav said he could marry us, because he's a ship captain," grinned Karl.

"So, will you marry me, my dear Inge?"

"Oh, yes indeed, my romantic and creative lover!" answered Inge.

Olav suggested they go to the small Lutheran church to conduct the marriage ceremony, and Helga quickly started a wedding invitation that spread in their small community near the mill. With her prompting, the guests also brought refreshments for the reception after the "wedding."

With the Lutheran pastor assisting, Olav pronounced Karl and Inge "husband and wife," and Karl kissed the bride. And they all adjourned to the fellowship room, where the bride and groom received congratulations and best wishes. And they happily joined with the others in enjoying the improvised refreshments—including a wedding cake hastily prepared by Helga.

Then, in their "bridal suite," Karl and Inge laughed and hugged and kissed, until their excitement grew as they coupled in a lusty first night of wedded bliss.

The next morning, Olav announced that the congregation wants to celebrate your marriage properly at the Sunday worship service and with a reception afterward, because more members want to be part of this unusual wedding.

"I hope you aren't too tired after your first night of marriage," he said, with a slight grin, as Helga looked down shyly. "You probably went right to sleep, after such as busy day," he added, as his grin grew wider.

"We did go to bed quickly," responded Karl, with his own grin, "and we enjoyed your comfortable bed immensely."

"And we look forward to enjoying your bed again," smiled Inge, "as soon as possible."

Parishioners filled the church in honor of the newlyweds from Skåne, and the pastor shared a relevant Christian message. Then he gave Karl and Inge their official marriage document.

Many of their "new friends" wished them well and were eager to learn more about the visiting artists. Karl explained that they came to study the pulp and paper process, so several men said they worked at the mill and looked forward to showing their part of the manufacturing.

Inge thanked all for making the wedding so special and so enjoyable.

Later, she praised Olav and Helga. "I don't think any other wedding ceremony could even come close to this wonderful experience!"

To thank them, Karl presented them with a colored sketch of them in front of the tugboat.

"We've never had a picture like that!" said Helga. "And to think we know the artist who drew this pleasing scene!"

In their bedroom, Karl and Inge chuckled about their unique experience. "I couldn't have dreamed up a more delightful wedding, and I can hardly wait to share our experience with my family and friends."

"You'd better ease into the story, so they don't collapse in shock," smiled Karl. He hugged and kissed her, and they repeated their passionate lovemaking of the night before.

As they toured the mill the next day, they saw several of their new friends on the job. They both sketched the workers and the equipment as their guide led them through the mill.

In the research lab, they learned about the many techniques for making paper, and the technicians pointed out some of the special combinations of pulp, as well as the various coatings being used and being considered in making paper.

The plant manager and the director of the lab found Karl's interest in pulp as an art medium surprising and intriguing. And they offered suggestions about treating the pulp so it would hold the embossing and debossing Karl described.

"You might find that our experiments with special paper will connect with art as well," said the lab director. "Right now, we're experimenting with our paper used for photography. We don't do the special coating of the photo paper, but we do have a lab for testing by developing photos. We'd be glad to work with you if you want to try our darkroom to print photos."

"Sorry to say, but we don't even have a camera, because I couldn't bring my new Kodak 35mm camera to Sweden," said Karl, with regret.

"We can lend you one—a 35mm Leica from Germany, with a light meter and flash," said the director, to a surprised Karl. "It's an extra set, so consider it a permanent loan. In exchange, you can help us test our paper by taking photos for us to process."

"And we can report back to the University about the value of this kind of paper for use in art," said Inge. "This might generate keen interest, because photography has displaced much of the traditional representational painting. Now photography has emerged as an art medium itself."

The next day, the Director of Forestry started his tour at the nursery, where he explained the development of hybrid trees. Then they meandered through clusters of trees of various ages, ending up well into the forest of full-grown conifers—as Karl and Inge tried out the Leica.

Later, the lab processed the film, so Karl and Inge could try enlarging their photos.

"Good work," said the Director when he saw the results. "Our company might want to use your photos, if that's okay by you."

"Fair enough," said Karl, and Inge agreed.

Their visit took on a modern twist the following day, when Oskar Tostenson, the Dolman Vice President of Operations, dropped in—by plane. He explained that he intended to fulfill his promise made during their meeting in Stockholm. If willing, they could join him in a flight to see the vast scope of the company holdings.

Karl noticed that the forests seemed sometimes splotchy because of the terrain and the climate, but the extent of the holdings impressed him.

The pilot took the plane to a high altitude, and he told about the importance of Sweden to Germany. Way beyond the view from the plane, explained the pilot, convoys of German trucks and rows of rail cars are hauling a variety of products, including iron ore from Kirona in Sweden to Narvik on the coast of Norway.

Though Karl had heard of the German transportation system in the north, he hadn't expected such a major network. He made mental notes to discuss later with Haaken and Kjell, so he could better understand how they might help the Norwegians sabotage the German transportation system.

Oskar explained that the Gulf Stream in the Atlantic Ocean kept the Narvik harbor free of ice in the winter. The harbors in that area, he added, allow the German air and sea defense to attack Allied shipping to Russia. He also described how the Germans were building massive concrete gun emplacements along the west coast of Norway to protect their own vital shipping corridor from British air and sea attacks.

"We don't dare go near the coast, of course," said Oskar, "or the Germans would turn their weapons on us."

After the plane landed near the mill, Oskar said that he needed to fly back to Stockholm, and he offered Karl and Inge a ride so they could take the train from Stockholm. They quickly bid thanks and farewell to Olav and Helga, as well as several others. Then, when the plane flew over the mill, the pilot wagged the wings of the plane.

"Great salute for a revealing and joyful visit!" said Karl.

"We heard that you turned your visit into a surprise wedding that involved most of the mill community," smiled Oskar. "Well, our company prides itself on providing good service."

"The folks there certainly served us well," said Inge. "We'll cherish forever our unique wedding. And we enjoyed our unusual but delightful honeymoon!"

Before Karl and Inge left Stockholm, they thanked Oskar for the enlightening—and romantic—experience, and Karl presented him a series of drawings of the Dolman mill, harbor and forests.

"Terrific! These certainly capture the essence of our operations, and in such a beautiful way," said Oskar. "They will soon hang in our offices as a warm reminder of your special visit."

Inge told of her interest in industrial design, and she appreciated the protective housing on the machines and the efficient systems in the production process.

"We might want more of your observations in the future," said Oskar, "because we work constantly to achieve safety and efficiency."

Art Sleuths

On the train back to Lund, Karl and Inge reflected about their interesting "art research."

"Married life certainly proved interesting, too," said Inge, "with your dramatic proposal, our unique wedding, and, of course, our bliss in bed."

"When the university session finishes, we should continue our honeymoon," said Karl. "I've been thinking that a leisurely ride on the western part of the Göta Canal could provide a pleasant and romantic way to be together."

"I vote for that," said Inge. "Maybe somewhere along the way, we could catch a performance by our popular singer, Evert Taube, who even protests the Nazis in his folk music. And he generally pays tribute to a popular Swedish composer, Carl Michael Bellman—which would contrast to the grim plays by Strindberg.

"And, I imagine you would like to combine art with some research related to access of information about Norway."

"Well, the romantic part appeals to me," said Karl. "And I suppose we could check out the German influence on shipping at Gothenburg," said Karl. "We could go by ship from Helsingborg to start our surveillance. Maybe we could get a look at the wartime production at the Volvo facilities in Gothenburg, too."

"I think Dad, and Kjell, could arrange that," said Inge.

"My dual life—now yours too—means that even a honeymoon could conceal some spying, besides offering opportunity for art...and music...and love," said Karl.

"You've talked me into it," laughed Inge. "I love your ideas...and you!"

Another surprise awaited them in Lund. When they got off the train, a large group of family and friends greeted them.

Inge rushed to hug her mother, who hugged her back and exclaimed: "Welcome home, Mrs. Nelson!"

"How did you know?" laughed Inge. "We thought we would share our wonderful secret with you in person!"

"The pastor who officiated at your wedding ceremony couldn't wait to tell our pastor," explained Hanna. "He told about how the members of his congregation turned out for the event and provided a festive wedding reception for you. And he said that the captain of the tugboat also officiated at your wedding."

"Oh yes, that's how Karl arranged for our wedding," said Inge. "He's full of creative ideas, so he said our new friend the tugboat captain could help launch our marriage. And what an exciting and joyful time it was…and is!

"Maybe now we could repeat the wedding in a more formal way at our church," said Inge, apologetically.

"That would be wonderful," said Hanna, "but most of all, we're thankful for your happiness with such an outstanding husband!"

Tore also hugged his daughter, and said, "You do succeed in surprising us…this time in a big way. But your mother and I think you've chosen the right direction for your life. Anja and Jakob, of course, admire your creative wedding and are thrilled to have Karl in our family."

Tore and Hanna repeated their thoughts and feelings to Karl, as they welcomed him into the family. "We know you and Inge face extra risks in your future, but we also know how capable both of you are," said Tore.

"Now, we have a surprise for you!" Tore announced. "We got a new Volvo for you. We picked it up for you in Malmö, where it came right from the factory in Gothenburg."

"What a great surprise!" exclaimed Inge, as she hugged an equally surprised Karl. Then she hugged her dad and mother.

"This one will require some extra attention," explained Tore, "because it runs on gas generated by a wood-burning attachment."

"I never heard of that kind of gas," said Karl.

"You might say gasoline is Sweden's Achilles' heel," explained Tore, "because we produce so little. But we do have wood!"

"Well, with our association with Dolman, we should be able to get an ample supply of wood to burn," said Karl, "but we'll sure need a lot of advice about operating this kind of vehicle."

Finally, the faculty of the Art and Architecture Department, and fellow students of Karl and Inge, took their turn in congratulating the newlyweds. Jenny appeared a bit saddened by their marriage, but she praised them for their choice of the research topic...and for their choice of each other.

"You two certainly thrive on creative actions," said Prof. Lindhof. "What an admirable way to combine art research and imaginative romance!"

Dr. Johansson complimented them for adding a new element in art history, and, he said, "I look forward to hearing your impressions from your study of contemporary art materials. And the students and

I will also be curious about your inspired romance in a mill town.

"We anticipate a full house again when you're ready to tell about your unusual project."

When Karl reached Haaken and Kjell on the radio, they too congratulated Karl and Inge. "Glad you made the connection," said Haaken, "because you were made for each other. And we welcome you, Inge, to our team. Sorry about the secrecy that caused extra tension for you when you learned of Karl's double life.

"Now, the two of you have an even better double-life," said Kjell.

Then Karl and Inge shared the information they had gathered, including the German shipping activities visible from the tugboat and their information about the German transportation system to Norway across northern Sweden.

Karl suggested a continued study of the shipping pattern, if they could be passengers on a Swedish merchant ship from Helsingborg to Gothenburg. "From there, we might have a chance to go up to Oslo for a report from Norway."

"We'll see what we can arrange," said Kjell.

"We relayed to your parents the news of your marriage, Karl," said Haaken. "They thought the unusual wedding fit your creative approach to life, so they didn't seem surprised that a tugboat captain helped with the ceremony. Fitting for a family involved in shipping, said your dad. And they, of course, send their congratulations and best wishes to you and Inge. They look forward to getting acquainted with you, Inge, although they know much already because of descriptions provided by us, as well as by Karl's glowing comments.

"Anxiety in America increases every day, with more of the world involved in war," added Haaken. "The role of our agency will no doubt intensify, and your foothold in Sweden could turn out to be strategic. Meanwhile, keep up the good work at the university, and for us. Both of you should be due soon to receive your doctor's degrees, which should add to your credibility for our work. So we look forward to congratulating you for that attainment."

Chapter 18: ART INVESTIGATION

At the beginning of the summer of 1941, Haaken and Kjell called Karl and Inge in for a special meeting.

"Leaders of the Allied countries, as well as neutral United States and Sweden, have a new concern, even at this stage of the conflict," said Haaken. "They fear that when the war ends, assuming that Germany will eventually fall, the Nazi leaders could evade prosecution for war crimes that might be too vague to pin down.

"So we—Kjell and I—have recommended pursuing less-important but more-specific crimes," said Haaken. "We want to get evidence about theft of valuable art and jewelry by Nazi leaders. They've already launched a systematic plunder of property belonging to wealthy Jews. We can't stop that atrocity, but maybe we can document it for future courtroom evidence.

"Karl, you probably remember how the FBI helped convict some of the Prohibition-era gangsters in the United States," prompted Haaken.

"Oh yes, I remember the irony," grinned Karl. "The FBI couldn't develop a provable case about murder and other crimes of that degree, so they nailed the crime bosses with income-tax evasion.

"I get it," continued Karl. "You want evidence about lower-level crime—just in case. Art theft might be your version of income-tax evasion."

"That's it, and we want your help," said Haaken. "Fresh with your PhD's, you should be well suited for that kind of spying. That means you'll be on our payroll, too, Inge—and subject to the risks of spying as the wife of an American. Hope you're willing and ready for the challenge."

"I don't quite understand the tax story, but I do get the message about collecting information and evidence related to stealing art and other valuables," said Inge. "And where Karl goes, I go!"

"We think you'll make a great team," said Kjell, "but watch your back—all the time.

"You friend Jenny has been snooping around rather boldly, trying to get more information about you, Karl, in particular. We've tossed in some red herrings to divert her. I think she found that your continuing association with Dolman was a dead end," said Kjell.

"Now, maybe we can turn her suspicions into a helping hand for you, because we want you to continue your study of paper and publishing in Denmark, and, of all places, in Germany.

"Part of your cover will be your association with Dolman, so you'll be conducting business about pulp and paper. A few executives there know and approve of your mission. Dolman will provide you business cards and customer contacts. Needless to say, your PhD's should be very impressive on those cards!

"France offers the best hope for information, because the French Resistance is fanatical in their hate of the Nazis, so they might help you get specifics about how the Nazis took every valuable they could grab."

Then Haaken added: "If Jenny Henriksson continues true to form after we plant some information, she might pave your way by alerting the Nazis to accommodate you—while trying to get the goods on you, so to speak."

"Who knows—with Hitler's interest in art and architecture, you might even get a chance to meet him. And his architect, Albert Speer, might be interesting and valuable for you to meet. That, of course, could open the door for getting information at lower levels of the Third Reich," said Haaken.

"Yes, we found out that the Germans like to brag about their triumphs, especially to an American," said Karl. "That trait could help us get information we want."

Karl and Inge got lots of attention as they drove to Stockholm—at least their strange Volvo got attention. In Stockholm, they located the apartment provided by Dolman—for the record, anyway.

The next day, Hans Svenstrom, their mentor at Dolman, met them at the company headquarters. He introduced them to several top executives, showed them their office, and then he escorted them to the Product Development Department.

"Here's where you'll learn the ropes of our business," said Hans, as he introduced Karl and Inge to the development team.

"What's in here will be your bible about our company," he said, as he handed each a handsome black briefcase.

"This certainly looks impressive!" exclaimed Inge, as she saw her named stamped in gold: "Dr. Inge Lindfelt, Graphics Consultant."

Karl nodded in appreciation as he saw his name on his briefcase and noted the attractive tabulated contents.

"The printing companies you'll visit expect quality—the Germans in particular, with their proud link to Guttenberg," explained Hans. "They also respond well to rich-looking materials," he added, with a smile, "and to doctor's degrees. And I think they will be impressed, Inge, by your credentials. And your good looks—both of you—will appeal to them," he added shyly.

"As we go through the information, you'll note that we show several examples of elaborate printed pieces. And the Germans in particular—and especially the Nazis—like the dazzle of ornate design.

"Germany dominates the printing business, especially now," explained Hans, "so, for more than one reason, you will be targeting companies and government agencies there.

"To start your orientation and training, we'll walk through the contents in your briefcase now," continued Hans. "Then your teammates here in our Development Department will spend the next few days discussing the trends and details of the printing business. Your training in design, of course, gives you a running start, so I look forward to reports about your progress. Then we'll send you on the road—where your Volvo should help you make a dramatic impression."

The next few days proved to be an intensive education, starting with the various characteristics of printing paper: strengths, textures, sheet and roll sizes, grain directions, calendaring, coatings and colors.

Then they shifted to letterpress, lithography and offset lithography, intaglio and screen printing. That led to study of type fonts, rules, dies, embossing and blind embossing, debossing, stamping of foil, binding, and even trimming and die-cutting as part of design. They learned about the preparation of various types of printing plates. Other nuances surfaced as their study progressed.

Karl and Inge both felt more at home with the exploration of inks and the colors they produced on differing kinds and colors of paper.

After absorbing much of this information and reviewing it over meals, during sightseeing ventures and in the evenings in their apartment, they gained enough confidence to discuss printing in its broad scope as well as detailed applications with their mentors in the Development Department.

Finally, Karl and Inge faced the challenge of participating in a mock meeting with a customer, as they offered advice and options suited to the stated printing purpose. Then they participated in an exercise about estimating cost and completing an order with specifics about the finished product and shipping arrangements.

After that, Hans and other Dolman executives and members of the Development Department honored Karl and Inge with an informal graduation ceremony. Hans smiled as he awarded them a "first-of-the-kind" Dolman Graphics Consultant diplomas.

While receiving the congratulations, they shared their appreciation for the excellent training.

"We think our new knowledge will serve us far into the future," said Karl.

"Of course, we hope it will serve us well in our immediate future, too," said Inge, as she anticipated their coming challenge of gathering secret information about the theft of art by the Nazis.

Chapter 19: JOB—SALES REPRESENTATIVES

To start their "grand tour" of Europe as Graphics Consultants, Karl and Inge repeated their visit to Copenhagen, this time to meet with a major publisher. They soon learned that "freedom of the press" no longer existed there, as the Nazis watched the operation carefully. But they did get a request for more information about the paper needed for that "captive enterprise."

Then they drove to Hamburg to contact printers there. They pushed on to meet with a publisher in Bremen, as they began to feel more confident in their work. When they visited with the workers in the printing plants, they primed the pump to get scuttlebutt about art being accumulated by the Nazi leaders.

Their circuit included Hannover and Brunswick, and they finished at Berlin.

Berlin proved to be an interesting city to visit—including an outstanding art museum. There they got hints from the guards about the possibility of new art expected at the museum. And they quietly collected names and notes for future follow-up.

They did meet with Nazis involved in publishing, but not Hitler or Speer. Of course, Karl and Inge impressed those lower-level Nazis with their titles, style and knowledge. The Nazis even praised them for their desirable Germanic physical stature and good looks.

On their way back to Stockholm, they met in Malmö with Haaken and Kjell. They apologized for the lack of useful information about stolen art. But both Haaken and Kjell expressed satisfaction with their gambit in Germany—and the hints of more information possible later.

At Dolman, Hans welcomed them back, and their orders for paper surprised and pleased him and others at the company. The folks in the Development Department greeted them warmly, and they felt gratified as Karl and Inge provided details about their consulting success.

Haaken and Kjell allowed Karl and Inge some time to relax and recover, but they expressed their concern that the window of opportunity in Europe might be closing soon. They predicted a squeeze on travel and increased risk for an American, as the United States had recently stepped up its help to Britain.

"We want you to travel to Paris as soon as possible, before the Nazis shut the door in your face. Or, worse, arrest you on some pretext. You could be in big trouble, and so could our quest for evidence," explained Haaken.

So Karl and Inge quickly scheduled consulting meetings in Paris, and traveled there directly by train. The Paris they saw still seemed like the "life of the party"—on the surface. But in the "underground," activities to resist the Nazis were flourishing.

"I think we've struck gold," said Karl, after a careful and courageous customer helped make the connection to stolen art.

They were able to collect a lode of evidence about art taken from Jews in France and beyond.

But, anticipating the challenge to take the information back to Sweden, Karl and Inge carefully worked their data into orders for paper, and into special instructions about shipping and billing. They also concealed more information in summaries of requests for follow-up by their company.

Their mnemonic code proved to be simple to prepare...and they hoped it would be adequate for producing a detailed report later. Still, they worried about getting the information past the Germans.

"Maybe it will be too boring even for the most diligent Germans to spend much time analyzing it," said Karl, hopefully.

As a bonus, of course, they had generated actual interest by French customers about purchasing printing paper.

Karl and Inge sensed, as anticipated, that the Nazis were continually tracking their journey. But many German officers they met in restaurants turned out to be cordial and curious. They flirted with Inge, but they paid more attention to Karl, as they sought information about America. Several were eager to talk with him when they learned that he was from Wisconsin, where they had relatives.

Only one incident marred their association with the Germans. A strutting and aggressive member of the Hitler Youth Corps tried to argue with Karl, who didn't respond. Nearby officers watched with interest.

When loud and abusive words didn't provoke Karl, the German Youth start to poke and push. Suddenly Karl pivoted on his left foot, slammed his right foot into the side of the knee of the young Nazi and swung his right hand hard against his neck. As the young man hit the floor with a thud, the other Germans clapped in appreciation.

When an officer commented to Inge that Karl must have had good military training, she remembered the answer: "Oh, he grew up with Indians in Wisconsin, and they trained him well."

When that answer spread among the other officers, they were eager to know more, so Karl embellished descriptions of his Ojibway friends and the skills he had learned from them.

Back at their apartment in Stockholm, Karl and Inge deciphered their information hidden in orders and inquiries for paper products. Then they outlined the information they had collected about the confiscation of art by the Nazis. As anticipated, the French Resistance had proven to be the best source of information—with their promise to collect more evidence about the Nazi art theft through their network across Europe.

The next day in their office at the Dolman headquarters, Karl and Inge passed along to the Marketing Department the orders and inquiries they had accumulated.

Then, in the company conference room, they met with Haaken and Kjell, as well as the company representative, Hans Svenstrom.

Though Karl and Inge apologized again for their limited success in gathering data, Haaken and Kjell expressed great appreciation for this important early information—and the connection with the French underground.

"Remember the income-tax comparison," said Haaken. "We want just enough evidence to have an ace up our sleeve in case other prosecution fails."

"After we analyze your information and procedures, we can meet again to consider strategies and tactics for your next ventures," said Kjell. "Who knows, you might even generate some more orders for Dolman paper."

"We're not sure about the risk," said Haaken. "We presume the Germans tracked your every move. Still, you probably confused them. With their obsession for regimented procedures, they may still be scratching their heads about a husband and wife team, with doctor's degrees, selling paper while exploring art."

"Evidently, you impressed our customers favorably, so they should welcome you back," observed Hans.

"Now, while we plan your next move, you're free to take a little time off," said Haaken.

"Maybe you'll want go for a relaxing drive in that weird-looking Volvo," said Hans, with a smile. "We'll even provide the wood to burn."

Though Karl wished they could take the leisurely Göta Canal crossing of Sweden and then go to Helsingborg, they decided to drive directly there, instead. But still at a leisurely pace.

Jakob shouted for joy when he heard and saw the weird Volvo approaching, and he ran into the house to alert the rest of the family. So they all hurried out on the porch, waiting to greet Inge and Karl with hugs and kisses and handshakes.

"You sure look fit and happy!" said Tore. "And we thank God for your safety in these dangerous times!"

"And you're timing is perfect," said Hanna, "because dinner is ready. Anja, could you set two more plates, please?"

"Sure will!" said Anja. "I can hardly wait to hear about their adventures!"

When they returned to Stockholm, Haaken, Kjell and Hans greeted them with the announcement of another assignment.

"Evidently you've impressed our customers, just as we suspected, and the word of your consulting has spread," said Hans. "And that opens up further opportunity for our business...but more important, for your search for evidence about Nazi plunder."

"We just learned that an underground source at Brandenburg may have information about *kristallnacht*, when the Nazis raided Jewish businesses and homes in 1938 and confiscated everything of value," said Haaken.

"So, we hope you're refreshed, because it's time to stoke up your Volvo and make the German circuit again," he said.

"Sounds good," said Karl, as Inge nodded in agreement. "Great cities, great scenery, great food...even some fine folks to do business with."

"This does seem like a special opportunity," said Kjell, "but security may be getting a bit dicey. We learned that your friend Jenny has intensified the probe of your activity. So be extra vigilant this time."

"We have some repeat business for you in Hamburg, and then you could go down to a new consultation with a publisher in Brandenburg," explained Hans. "And that company works with printers in Berlin, which is not far away."

Once again, their Volvo got lots of attention…some from officials and other folks who recognized it from a prior drive through Denmark and Germany.

In Hamburg, the managers and those in the shop welcomed them like old friends. In a demonstration of graphics, a type compositor ran off a proof for them. Karl noticed the bottom of the sheet was folded. He saw some notes written there, so he folded the proof and put it in his briefcase for later examination.

After they met with the executives of the publishing company in Brandenburg, they toured the plant and saw a magazine coming off the press. Near the end of the tour, the foreman of the binding operation handed Inge a finished copy of the women's magazine. As she glanced through the magazine, she spotted a handwritten note, so she casually closed the magazine and slid it into her briefcase.

They participated in a productive meeting in Berlin, with a discussion about the satisfactory quality of the Dolman stock used for the cover and the pages of an outdoor sports magazine. The manager of the shipping department proudly showed that state-of-the-art operation. Then the foreman reached into the waste bin to retrieve a magazine for Karl. The manager pointed out that the sample didn't have a mailing label, and he explained that despite the modern addressing system, the machine sometimes misses a beat.

Karl thanked the foreman for the sample and added it to his briefcase.

In their hotel room, they discussed their meetings and the stories in the magazine samples.

"Looks like the French Resistance alerted the labor unions about our investigation, so we're getting some surprising clues and in surprising ways," whispered Karl.

Without taking a chance by talking more about their new evidence from the proof sheet and the magazines, they again "coded" the data into Holmen printing estimates and information inquiries.

At dinner, Inge got Karl's attention: "Look who's here...one of the Germans in our classes at the University."

"He's spotted us and is coming over," responded Karl.

"Good to see some friendly foreigners!" exclaimed Gerhart Bayer. "Remember me from the university?"

"Sure do," said Karl. "Your information about printing technology has helped us in our present work."

"How does that connect with your being in Berlin?" asked Gerhart.

"We both represent Dolman," said Inge, as she handed a business card to Gerhart. "My card doesn't indicate it, but I'm actually married to this guy," smiled Inge, while Karl offered his card.

"Both with doctor's degrees! You have done well!

"I remember when you conducted that outstanding research with the paper company," said Gerhart, "That paid off, evidently, in this challenging economy."

"So far, it's paying off quite well," said Karl, "thanks to some good orders from here in Germany."

"Might we join you for dinner?" asked Gerhart.

"We'd enjoy that…but who is 'we'?" asked Inge.

"I'll find Janna and bring her over," Gerhart answered. "I think we all have a lot in common."

He returned with a lovely blonde on his arm. "Janna, meet two of my schoolmates from Lund University—Inge Lindfelt and Karl Nelson. Both outstanding artists…and now representing a Swedish paper company.

"Janna Bremen is a graduate student here in Berlin, in marketing," said Gerhart, as he introduced her.

"We sure do have a lot in common," said Inge, as she told of their work with the paper company.

"You look like you fit in here, both of you," said Janna, "but Gerhart said you're an American, Karl."

"Don't hold that against me," laughed Karl. "I'm an American of Swedish descent. That's probably the only reason Inge married me."

"That, and a thousand other good reasons," laughed Inge.

"How about you, Gerhart? Still involved in art?" asked Karl.

"Like so many in Germany these days, I'm basically a government bureaucrat," said Gerhart.

"Some bureaucrat!" said Janna. "He works in architectural planning for the city."

"Great coincidence," said Inge, "because Karl said he would like to meet your top architect."

"You mean Albert Speer?" asked Gerhart.

"That's the name," said Inge.

"Well, well, the coincidence becomes more remarkable, because he's the boss at the top of our organization, and he's here tonight," said Gerhart. "I know him, but not well. But I'll see if there's a chance for you and Karl to meet him. And while I'm gone, you can bet Janna will ask about America."

"As part of my graduate study, I'm writing a report about our Berlin art museum," said Janna, "so I'm curious about your New York Metropolitan Museum. Have you visited there, Karl?"

"Yes, and it's huge and magnificent...like your Berlin museum," said Karl.

"I've visited the New York museums, too," said Inge, to the surprise of Janna.

"When I studied at the Minneapolis Art Academy for a year," continued Inge, "I also saw several other great art museums in America, such as Chicago's, before I returned to Sweden."

"What a marvelous experience that must have been!" exclaimed Janna. "I hope I get the chance sometime."

"From what we learned, your Berlin collection seems to be expanding," said Karl.

"Rapidly," said Janna, "as Germany moves much art from private collections to Berlin, so the public can enjoy the paintings and sculpture.

"We can talk about that more later, because here comes Gerhart," said Janna. "By the smile on his face, I'd say he has found his boss."

"Come quickly," said Gerhart, when he reached their table, "so you can at least say hello to Albert Speer. They'll save our table for us."

Karl grabbed the Leica. "Just in case," he said to Gerhart.

Albert Speer moved from his table toward them as they approached. "What a treat," he said. "I heard we might talk about art and architecture for a few minutes. So I welcome the refreshing change from discussing factories."

Gerhart introduced the three of them, explaining that Janna studies Management of Art in Berlin, and that Karl is an outstanding American artist and architect who just got his doctor's degree at Lund University. And," added Gerhart, with a smile, "there he captured the heart of his wife Inge. She's Swedish and also received her doctor's degree in design at Lund University."

"You have impressive friends, Gerhart," said Speer, "in more ways than one," as he glanced from Inge to Janna.

"We've learned about the remarkable style and scope of your architectural planning," said Karl. "And we heard about your use of strong design to inspire the public."

"Well, as you no doubt know, I benefit from having an appreciative and powerful client," said Speer, with a slight grin.

"I regret we can't talk longer," said Speer. "I'm pleased to meet you. Maybe we can talk more another time."

"Could we pose with you for a photo, if someone on your staff could take our picture?" asked Karl.

"Why not," said the startled Speer.

"Great Leica!" said the officer, as he took the picture.

Back at the table, they all expressed their amazement about the encounter, and Karl thanked Gerhart for making the connection.

Slowly, they came back down to earth and continued their previous conversation.

After a delicious and leisurely dinner, Karl announced that he and Inge still had homework.

"But not schoolwork," laughed Inge. "We just need to write up the orders and inquiries for paper we got here."

"Hope that kind of homework continues here for us, despite the war," said Karl. "And we've enjoyed being with both of you, so we too could share our similar interests.

"Incidentally, do you have business cards?" asked Karl. "Maybe we can get together again...for business and pleasure."

As they started their "homework," Inge remarked that "Gerhart and Janna are gracious as well as intelligent. They seem like the kind who could be our friends."

"What a shame," said Karl, "that war prevents that kind of friendship. But maybe we'll try to connect again, at least to learn more about the reasons behind the expansion of the art museum."

In the Dolman conference room, the report by Karl and Inge astounded Haaken, Kjell and Hans.

"This intelligence data alone makes your trip remarkable," said Haaken. "But I can hardly imagine the chance to meet Albert Speer—and take his picture! Well, you said you hoped to meet some top Nazis."

"We need to follow up as soon as we can," said Kjell, "but we can't appear too eager, or it might look suspicious. What do you think, Hans? Got any inquiries from Berlin or vicinity that need follow-up by Karl and Inge?"

"Well, the publisher in Hannover likes our stock…and likes our consulting team," said Hans. "They plan to reproduce some art as special prints, maybe for more government propaganda. Their printing specialists think that with your art background, Karl and Inge, your advice would be ideal."

"That would put you close again to Berlin," said Haaken, "and close again to your classmate there. But let's give it some time to simmer. We want to check out what mischief Jenny the spy is involved in. She knows your German classmate, too, and may be capitalizing on that connection."

After a couple of weeks, Haaken declared an "all clear" about Jenny.

"Fuel up your Volvo with a load of wood and head south again," said Haaken. "Maybe the art prints at Hannover will provide another connection to stolen art. For one thing, I suppose the Nazis don't expect to lose this war, so they may be a bit brazen in displaying their illegally obtained art. Maybe the folks in Hannover will leak some more information."

"Mind a delay of a day or two so we can drop in on Inge's family?" asked Karl. "Then we can take the ferry from there to Denmark. Our Volvo gets a lot of attention, so we might glean some more information from curious Danes about the progress of the German gun fortifications."

"A delay shouldn't be a problem," said Haaken. "As I said before, we don't want to seem too eager when you visit Hannover and Berlin."

Art Sleuths

In a repeat of previous visits, Inge and Karl got a warm welcome on a Saturday afternoon from her loving family—and eager curiosity, especially from Anja and Jakob.

Hanna soon set out coffee and pastries so the family could gather to hear about the consulting activities, especially in Germany.

Anja and Jakob cheered when Inge told about how Karl subdued a thug from the Hitler Youth Corps.

Tore and Hanna expressed surprise at their success as graphics consultants and their commissions from the orders for paper. And they could hardly believe that Inge and Karl had met a top Nazi leader…and got a photo with him.

Later, during dinner, Hanna asked about Karl's family: "Are you able to communicate with your parents so they know you are safe and sound?"

"The American consulate provides the only way we can exchange messages, so at least we know they remain healthy and active, and they know we are the same," said Karl. "We haven't shared information about our ventures in other parts of Europe, because that could raise a red flag with the Nazis and possibly limit our activity there."

"I'm sure eager to meet Karl's parents and other relatives and friends, but who knows when we will have a chance to go to America," said Inge. "I'd be interested in returning to Minneapolis, too, including a visit to the Art Academy."

During the worship service the next morning at the Lutheran church, they all felt hope and comfort in response to the prayers for safety and peace in the world. And they felt renewed by participating in the liturgy and music and sharing in communion.

The previous afternoon, Hanna had again invited relatives and friends to join in the impromptu family reunion. Then, besides telling about their travels to the south in Europe, Inge and Karl told about their own opportunities to paint, as they prepared for a show in Stockholm.

"Dad, you'd like some of Karl's paintings...well, 'conglomerations' might be a better term," explained Inge. "Good thing we can work in the Dolman shop, with our strange material

"As usual, he acquires damaged Masonite panels as his 'canvas', only sometimes he includes the damaged, ragged edges of his panels as part of the design. Next, he paints the panel with colorful geometric patterns. Then he places a circular saw blade or gear or tool where he wants it and sprays to create a shaded outline of the blade...or a series of silhouettes, you might say."

Tore didn't respond immediately. "I'm trying to visualize that," he said. "I certainly don't see it as the art I'm used to, but I do see it as art related to my life and work. So I'm interested."

"Inge creates in a similar yet different way," interjected Karl. "Only for her sculpture, she uses a cutting torch and welder to assemble three-dimensional abstract designs."

"With those skills," laughed Tore, "we might want you to help us create new some products at the plant, Inge."

"We should have an art show here," said Anja. "Maybe I could arrange it at our school and invite the whole community."

"Great idea!" said Hanna.

"We'll help," said Jakob, and several others offered to assist.

Later, when they climbed in their Volvo to go to Denmark, Tore inquired about the car's performance.

"It runs great," said Karl, "though getting fuel poses a challenge sometimes, so we burn coal and peat as well as wood."

"And we meet many people wondering about our strange and special vehicle," laughed Inge. "Sort of like our weird art, you might say."

In Hannover, the graphics specialists involved in producing art reproductions stated their surprise at and appreciation for the capabilities of Karl and Inge. So they all enjoyed the challenge of applying the latest methods and materials to achieve the desired printing results.

As a result of the discussions, Karl and Inge concluded that some of the art being copied came from the Nazi plundering of Jewish treasures. But when asked about the source of the original art, the German graphics specialists defended the art acquisition as the best way to protect and exhibit the paintings, prints and drawings. And they freely shared information about the Nazi department responsible for handling the art.

As an expression of their positive feelings toward Karl and Inge, the printing company leaders presented them with a high-quality set of reproductions from the test runs.

In Berlin, when they called Gerhart, he greeted them like long-lost friends. When he heard their schedule with the publisher, he urged them to stop by his office after they finished their consultation.

"I'm sure others in my office would like to talk with you about architecture and art," he said. "Later, Janna might have time to show you the additions we talked about at the museum."

"It's a deal," said Karl.

At the publishing plant, the foreman of the shipping department brought in a sample of another magazine about handicrafts for Karl.

"Thanks," said Karl, "just what I need to improve some of my woodworking and metal-crafting skills."

"Be sure to let me have a look, too. Maybe it includes some suggestions about welding," said Inge, as the foreman looked surprised and puzzled. "I do welding for some of my sculpture," explained Inge.

In Gerhart's office, his colleagues eagerly questioned them—especially Karl. They wondered in particular about American factories converting to the production of war goods, but Karl confessed to be out of touch because of the many months since he had been in the United States.

On the other hand, they proudly showed some of their drawings for factories of various purposes, and they explained that they had designed some to be built underground.

Then Gerhart shifted the conversation to art, as he explained his association with Karl and Inge at Lund University.

"Time for us to catch up with Janna, so she can show off the changes in the art museum," said Gerhart.

On the way, he laughed that he had interrupted his colleagues before they gave away military secrets.

Janna greeted them warmly, and she showed them a large exhibit area where workers were hanging paintings.

Karl and Inge each recognized three of them that had been reproduced for the art prints they received from the publisher.

Janna explained that the German government had recently acquired this museum, and it would open this wing for a public showing in a few days.

Karl asked if they had been in storage previously, awaiting display.

"In a way," said Janna. "They had been acquired from private owners recently. Much like the art in United States that had been acquired by wealthy benefactors and given to museums."

"And I understand that much of your art was donated as a tax write-off," said Gerhart.

"Yes, we've experienced some controversy about that," admitted Karl.

German officers swarmed the hotel restaurant, and Karl called Inge's attention to the SS insignia some of them displayed.

"We don't want to deal with those super police in any way," explained Karl. "Even our neutrality might be violated by them if they felt so inclined."

"Actually, maybe we do want to deal with them," added Karl, sarcastically, "because that part of the Nazi organization probably conducted the 'art acquisition' we learned about, starting with *kristallnacht.*"

When they started to leave after their dinner, they were blocked at the door. "You two don't sound

German, so we'd like to see your identification papers," said an officer, who seemed determined to harass them.

"Ah ha, why would a Swede and an American be here," inquired the officer. "Maybe spies from two neutral countries, who want to travel around Germany as they please. With a camera, too."

"We're here on business, helping supply your government's publishing activity," said Karl, as he kept a close grip on the passports and camera.

"I need to check those out," said the officer.

"No you don't," said Karl. "Let's check them out at our consulates. Or better yet, let's check them with one of your leaders. We just met with him a few nights ago."

"Who's that?" demanded the officer.

"Albert Speer," said Karl.

"Well, that might be too complicated to arrange right now, so we'll just let you go on your way," said the officer. "And when do you expect to leave our country?"

"Tomorrow morning, now that our business is done," said Karl.

"Back to America and Sweden?" taunted the officer.

"America might be a bit difficult these days, so we'll just drive to Sweden," said Karl.

"Drive carefully," said the officer, scornfully. "The highways can be dangerous."

Karl and Inge breathed a sigh of relief when they returned to their hotel room.

"I'll be glad to head for home," said Inge.

"First thing in the morning," said Karl.

"Good!" said Inge. "Those arrogant officers could cook up an excuse to detain us and make life miserable, even if we are from neutral countries."

"Fortunately, we don't have to conceal any information in our business forms this time," said Karl. "Wait, let me look at the handicrafts magazine for any hidden information," he added, as he riffled through the magazine.

"Here's a note, but we can just memorize the information," said Karl. "And I'll destroy the note by throwing it in the firepot on the Volvo."

In the morning, they withdrew from Germany.

"Sorry that the relaxing drive we expected has turned into a tense trip," said Karl.

Before Karl and Inge drove on the ferry at Helsingör, the German guards examined their luggage and their papers thoroughly.

At the sight of the papers and the camera, the guards announced that they might have to detain them while they got help in checking the camera and examining the documents about the shipments of paper.

"Well, we promised the paper would be delivered immediately to your government's publishing organization, so we need to arrange for the shipment," said Karl.

"We just met with one of your leaders a few nights ago, even took his photo with this camera, so be careful not to expose the film," continued Karl. "You might check with him about whether we can be trusted."

"Oh, who might that be?" asked one guard, disdainfully.

"Albert Speer," said Karl.

"Well," said another guard, "I suppose we shouldn't delay any shipment for our government. So go ahead before the ferry leaves."

Later that night, after they again got a comforting welcome by Inge's family, they told Tore and Hanna about the growing tension they experienced in Germany.

"Please don't take any more chances there," pleaded Hanna.

Tore added his concern: "I say the same thing, because the Germans don't hesitate to break the rules when they want to, so I hope you can stay in Sweden, at least until the tension eases."

"We already concluded that," said Inge, "after the scare we had."

"Let's take a break by connecting with part of my family in Sweden," said Karl. "When I first got here, I did have contact with one family on my Olsson side in Tomelilla. They're probably wondering whatever became of me. At that time, they offered to bring the clan together for a reunion there."

"I'd like to meet them," said Inge, "and it would be an interesting change from our travels. And a chance to learn more about who you are," she added, with a sly smile.

"Okay, I'll call and encourage the possibility of a reunion next weekend, on our way back to Stockholm," said Karl. "And I'll report in with Haaken, so he knows we are alive and well and on our way back."

In Tomelilla, the Olssons—now with many other names besides Olsson—came from several

167

communities, including Malmö, Tryde, Ystad, Eslov, Simrishamn, Lund, and Kristianstad.

Their ages, occupations, and interests varied.

But they all were curious about their American relative—and about his beautiful Swedish wife…who even has a doctor's degree.

The weird Volvo first aroused their curiosity. Then they wanted to know about Karl's family, location and activity in America.

His doctor's degree in art and architecture surprised them.

"That's one dimension that's been missing from our family," said his second-cousin, Ingrid, who arranged the gathering of the clan. "And now we have two artists. What a wonderful expansion of our interests!" she added.

"Not all your relatives have had a chance to learn about you two, so would you be willing to stand in front and tell more about yourselves?" asked Ingrid.

"After we eat, of course," she added, as she waved over the array of food set out in the community center.

"Okay, if you'll pardon my mixture of English and Swedish," Karl responded to Ingrid.

"Your Swedish sounds very good to me," said Ingrid. "It even has our distinctive Skåne sound," she added, with a smile and a touch on Karl's arm.

After the meal, Ingrid introduced Karl, so the others would be clear how he's related.

Then Karl told about his life in America and how his study of architecture at the University of Wisconsin led him to more study at Lund University.

"Now let me introduce you to a great addition to our family, my wife Inge Lindfelt," announced

Karl. "We share dedication to design, including our work together as graphics consultants representing Dolman.

"She caught my eye when I first met her, because she was wearing a welder's mask," which caused puzzled smiles around the room. "And what a treat I had when she raised her mask."

After they clapped for her, Inge thanked them for the privilege of being part of Karl's clan. "You'll notice I have the Skåne sound, too, because I'm from Helsingborg. And we met at Lund University—when, by the way, he also wore a welding mask. So I got a treat when your handsome relative raised his mask.

"Nor did we marry in a traditional way—because a tugboat captain performed the ceremony. Karl's idea, I might add," she explained, with a laugh, and Karl and the others joined in.

"Now that we've just finished a series of business meetings in Denmark, Germany and France, being home in Sweden feels good to us," said Inge. "When we return to Stockholm, we plan to relax and prepare for an art show in Helsingborg. So I invite you to come and look at Karl's weird paintings, as well as my more-dignified works of art," she said with a teasing smile.

"We'll let you know details later," said a happy Karl. "Now I want to thank all of you for coming here and making us part of my wonderful Swedish family."

At the start of their drive to Stockholm, Karl headed for the center of the town. "Ingrid told me that Tomelilla includes a Milles statue too, so we have to pay tribute to that."

"Of course," smiled Inge.

"By the way, I believe it's my turn to drive this goofy mobile," added Inge.

"You're welcome to it," said Karl, as they changed places in the Volvo.

"Now I can lean back and enjoy the beauty of the plains and the rolling hills of Skåne.

"Just like southern Wisconsin," he commented.

"And southern Minnesota," added Inge.

Then the terrain became more like northern Wisconsin and Minnesota, with lakes and forests and rocky pastureland. Finally, the meandering waterways of Stockholm provided another stage of Sweden's beauty.

"I feel like Nils Holgersson as he explored Sweden," said Inge. "That story sure captured our interest in school as it taught us about the geography and the flora and fauna of our country. We liked the castles, too, especially those in Skåne."

"My mother read that story to me, in Swedish, I'll have you know," said Karl. "And I loved the story, too, even if I didn't understand all the words," laughed Karl.

"We should read it again, together," said Inge.

"What fun that would be! And I should understand almost all the Swedish words now," said Karl.

In the Dolman conference room late Monday afternoon, the same quintet—Karl, Inge, Haaken, Kjell and Hans—gathered to review the latest foray into Germany.

Karl and Inge told of the growing tension they experienced in Germany, and they explained that their fortuitous introduction to Albert Speer helped them avoid further harassment and possible detention.

"But, as far as we know," added Karl, "the German officers didn't sense the nature of our activity beyond our consulting with publishers. Good thing they didn't suspect, because we did get another bit of valuable information stuffed in another sample of a magazine. We didn't take any chances with that, so we memorized the content and destroyed the note in the Volvo burner."

"Gerhart and Janna didn't indicate any suspicions," added Inge. "In fact, Gerhart joked that Janna might be giving away some military secrets as she gave background about her work at the museum.

"And I recall that you checked Jenny for any connection with Gerhart and Janna, and you came up with a zero."

"Right," said Kjell, "We may be just encountering increased German edginess related to the air attacks from Britain. So they may feel less receptive to visitors from neutral countries."

"You've been getting good leads and making important connections for the future, and we may have a growing collection of useful clues for possible prosecution some day," said Haaken. "But we need to analyze how you might continue your work so it's effective—and safe."

"You've provided a solid foundation for our marketing of paper in those countries," said Hans, "and now you could continue the relationships you've built without having to go back. With your understanding of the various printing challenges, you could provide practical and valuable counseling by phone. And maybe, in that way, get some more information about the theft of art."

"Activity will slow down this month anyway," continued Hans, "as focus turns toward Christmas."

"Ironic, isn't it," said Haaken. "A time of peace, but the pace of war increases."

Chapter 20: U.S. ENTERS THE WAR

A pounding on the conference door startled them, and Hans went to check. One of his colleagues shouted, "Japan just bombed the United States a few hours ago! Come and listen to the report on the radio right now!"

They all rushed to join a group of others clustered around a radio on one of the desks, and they heard the grim report about the bombing of the U.S. Naval Base at Pearl Harbor in Hawaii.

No one spoke, as they listened, stunned by the news.

After the news report ended, the quintet returned to the conference room, shocked about the tragic situation—for Hawaii, for the United States and for the world.

"I don't know what we can do right now," said Haaken. "Guess we can just go home and stay tuned for developments. Then we can take a look at our upside-down world in the morning."

With that bleak end of the workday, the quintet joined other somber folks leaving the building, wondering about the foreboding news and what will come next.

In their apartment, Karl and Inge sat quietly.

Finally, Karl spoke softly: "To think we were just talking about the contradiction of the peace of

Christmas in the middle of war. Baby Jesus, we do need you now, to help us face this new shock."

"I feel so bad for your country, and for the world," said Inge. "So I pray that the world will survive this calamity."

After they sat quietly for many minutes, Karl asked Inge if she'd like a glass of wine.

"Yes, maybe that would be soothing," she said. "Then we can have a sandwich later, and try to catch more news on the radio. Don't know what else we can do, except pray for divine intervention."

"Nothing much else," agreed Karl. "Even the phones will be jammed, no doubt, so not much point in trying to call anyone."

In the morning, the quintet in the conference room seemed bewildered by the expanding war, as they tried to look ahead in their lives.

Haaken spoke about his perceptions: "With America embattled by Japan, Germany will probably add to the chaos by declaring war on the United States, too. Personally, Karl and I, and Inge too, seem to be caught between a rock and a hard place. Basically, the three of us are part of the U.S. military.

"I'm quite sure our military leaders would like to keep us right here, with our eyes and ears open and our heads down.

"Kjell, what's your view of our situation?" asked Haaken.

"Our intelligence organization still needs you, and we all should be able to operate together covertly. Despite Sweden's neutrality, our country provides unofficial and undercover assistance in Norway, Denmark and Finland. So I think we should keep on until told otherwise."

Hans offered his opinion: "Going into Nazi territory would probably be next to impossible for you, Karl and Inge, but our company still can benefit from your knowledge of our customers and your creativeness about our products. So we also should be able to continue your consulting that way until we're told otherwise."

Following that assessment, Haaken, Kjell, Karl and Inge continued to analyze the intelligence accumulated and record it on written documents and on IBM punch cards.

The Dolman Development Department capitalized on the opportunity to meet with Karl and Inge to learn about new technology in printing presses being developed by the Heidelberg printing equipment company in Germany.

"Heidelberg anticipates more uses of rolls as well as sheets for higher-speed printing, which probably will call for changes in the fiber and coatings characteristics of paper. The company has also experimented with faster drying time of the printed product to match the higher speed of the presses," explained Karl. "They admit they have had to put out some fires in their trials with gas burners for drying."

"Thanks for alerting us," said Hans, "so we can adapt to coming advances in printing."

Chapter 21: WASHINGTON, D.C., THE YEAR 1943

But the Swedish status quo ended abruptly. Kjell relayed new orders to Karl and Inge—a transfer to the new Office of Strategic Services in Washington, D.C.

"The leader of the OSS had kept tabs on your capabilities and accomplishments," he explained. "He said that your help could contribute much as the OSS gets its feet on the ground. He also understands that your American-Swedish marriage could complicate your involvement.

"He laughed, though, that war creates some 'strange bedfellows,' but he's accepted that concern," added Kjell, with a smile about the "bedfellows."

"Because of your situation, he's officially arranged for you both to be dual citizens of Sweden and the United States.

"Now, I have to figure out how to fly you to America," said Kjell. "While I'm arranging that, why don't you bid goodbye to the folks here and in Skåne."

They finished their farewells at Inge's home in Helsingborg, where Inge's family hosted a sad send-off to America. But Inge assured all that they would return as soon as possible.

Then Kjell explained another dramatic twist in the situation. "You'll get a fast flight to Iceland, because the Swedish air force welcomed an excuse to test its new SAAB B18 bomber. So the air force alerted the German command at Narvik of the intent to fly over the transportation route across northern Sweden, out over the Atlantic and back.

"At more than 300 mph, the B18 should make the flight in on time—and avoid a chance encounter with the Luftwaffe. By the way, when you get to the American base in Iceland, you might want to look up an interesting person on the staff there—by the name of Leroy Anderson. Seems that he's a noted American composer who's fluent in Swedish and other languages, so he's a valuable military interpreter, too."

So Karl and Inge went by train to the SAAB operations at Linköping, and the B18 quickly flew them to Iceland as the first stop of their shuttle.

While waiting for an American transport plane to pick them up for the final leg of the flight, they did track down Leroy Anderson and enjoyed an interesting conversation with him. He immediately began talking with Inge in Swedish, which impressed her. He explained that he grew up in Massachusetts, but his parents were immigrants from Sweden.

"Mine too," said Karl in Swedish, which impressed Anderson.

When he learned more about Leroy, Karl mentioned how much he enjoyed *Jazz Pizzicato* when it came out as a record. Inge noted that Leroy accepted the compliment with quiet acknowledgement—in the style of Sweden.

Then they chatted about another Swedish-American composer, Howard Hanson, and his outstanding compositions, such as the *Nordic Symphony*.

After a call to board the transport, they thanked Anderson for the interesting conversation. "Hope to see you again back in America," said Karl.

On the plane, Inge commented about the complexity of this trip, in contrast to her previous crossings to and from Minnesota. Then Karl explained that his meandering route from Wisconsin to Sweden started with a flight to Canada, then to England and ended with a parachute drop into Sweden.

"If it's all the same to you, I'd rather skip the parachute drop," smiled Inge.

"I'm with you...once was enough for me," laughed Karl.

In Washington, they settled in a small apartment provided by the OSS and soon participated in an orientation program, where they told of their experiences in Nazi-occupied territory. Their focus on art surprised and puzzled some from the newly reorganized OSS, but they quickly understood the significance after the comparison to the FBI's use of income-tax evasion to convict Prohibition criminals.

Before they began their fulltime duty, they explained to their new leaders that Karl had been away on his intelligence assignment for many months, and Inge had not had a chance to meet his family. Their plea proved convincing, because they were even lent an unmarked Plymouth sedan for the trip.

"And it won't even have to burn wood to run," laughed Karl, and his colleagues looked puzzled.

Inge explained that because of the extreme gas shortage in Sweden, they had to generate gas for their Volvo by the use of a special wood burning attachment.

They accepted the explanation…but still looked puzzled.

After Karl's parents recovered from the shock of a phone call from him, they suggested that they travel to Richland Center and meet them at Bill's home there.

"We don't want you to get stalled by snow up our way," said Bengt, "so I'll alert Bill and his family. They will be as happy as we are to see you again—and meet Inge."

Though light snow covered the ground much of the way to Wisconsin, no blizzards hindered their drive. Inge, however, expressed surprise, because the snow exceeded what Skåne usually received. So Karl did his best to describe the difference between a snowfall and the power and problems of a blizzard.

When they pulled up at Uncle Bill's, a large group rushed out of the house to meet them, led by Tina. After she hugged Karl, she hugged Inge as Karl introduced her to everyone.

"I think I know her already," laughed Tina, "and I think the others share that feeling from your few letters, Karl."

"Well, I have the advantage," said Inge, "because Karl told me so much already…but I'm elated to be here in person with his family…my new family."

Bengt followed suit with hugs for Karl and Inge, as did Bill and Kirsten.

Then Karl marveled at the size of Eric and the beauty of Ingrid, when they joined in the warm welcome.

"I imagine you're hungry and tired," said Kirsten. "So we'll deal with the hunger first, and while we eat, we can catch up on your life, Karl, and get even better acquainted with you, Inge."

During dinner, Ingrid exclaimed: "You look and sound so wonderful, Inge. Just like I imagined."

Gradually, Karl and Inge shared some of their experiences. Inge told about her family, and Karl reported about the gathering with the relatives in Sweden.

Bengt and Bill both expressed surprise at the degree Karl and Inge had been involved in intelligence activity in Nazi territory.

"I guess you actually were spies, weren't you?" asked Eric.

"Yes, in a way," said Karl, "though probably not as dramatic as you might think. But we did deal with several Nazi officers, including one high in the organization."

Later, as the conversation began to wind down, Ingrid announced with pride and pleasure: "You get to sleep in my room. I hope you'll be comfortable."

"I already feel comfortable, because all of you make me feel so much at home," said Inge.

"Sleep in as long as you want," said Kirsten, "because Saturday morning is usually rather leisurely here. But let me ask now about Sunday," she continued. "Many others in the community want to see you, and church might serve that purpose, if you'd like to go with us."

"Wouldn't miss it!" said Karl.

"I can hardly wait," said Inge.

The give and take of conversation continued over breakfast, and Karl and Inge told about their study at Lund University.

"Dad, you'll appreciate my first encounter with Inge," said Karl. "She wore a welder's mask, and what a treat I had when she raised the mask."

"That sounds so romantic!" exclaimed Ingrid.

"I can visualize that," laughed Bengt, "but what were you welding, Inge?"

"I studied sculpture, and I create what you might call modern art," explained Inge. "Some of my sculpture calls for welding pieces together."

"Sounds like Karl," said Bill, "when he used my welder to create art. Maybe the two of you can create something for us. Someday, that is."

Tina smiled with pride when Inge told about Karl's success at Lund.

"The faculty and students loved his art and his explanations of unusual paint and his strange 'canvas'."

"I'll bet he was still salvaging Masonite," laughed Bengt.

"I was still too poor to afford canvas," explained Karl. "Besides, Inge and I had a great time at the waterfront, scrounging for Masonite panels."

After breakfast, with Ingrid walking with Inge and Eric with Karl, they trudged through the snow to tour the town.

Karl asked if George Sandstrom still operated THE BREV.

"Sure does," said Ingrid. "And will he be surprised to see you again, Karl!"

After his initial shock, George welcomed them—to share in hot chocolate, "just like the old days," he said. Then he added: "I'm so sorry about Karla. I still miss her and think of her."

"I do, too," said Karl. "Me too," said Ingrid.

Then Karl changed the tone of the conversation. "Meet my wife, Inge Lindfelt. We both studied art at Lund University. And you'll probably sense a similarity to Karla."

"Yes, I do," said George. "And I'm happy to know you, Inge. And I welcome this chance to tell about Karl's art show here in town."

Then, as they sipped hot chocolate, they laughed about the art show, which was even featured in a radio broadcast, explained George.

Later, Ingrid had arranged for her and Karl to visit with the Lindstroms.

"How wonderful to see you, Karl," said Elin, as she greeted him at the door and hugged him. "Kirsten told me that you finally got back."

Then Henrik put both his hands on Karl's as he shook hands and drew Karl into the house.

"I am so sad about Karla," said Karl, "and I apologize that I couldn't return for her funeral—or even talk with you directly."

"We understand," said Elin, with tears in her eyes, "because your secret service contacted us and explained the situation. We're so grateful for the support from your family during this tragic time.

"We still miss her so much."

"So do I," said Karl, "and I'm so filled with regrets. She was so wonderful! And so is your family."

"He wanted me to bring him here to see you," said Ingrid, "because Karin and I helped bring them together. Is Karin here now?"

"No," said Elin, "she and Andrew both went skating, but they'll be in church in the morning. I think Anja and Dan are home for the weekend, so they should be at church, too."

"Could you stay for a cup of coffee, Karl? And some hot chocolate, Ingrid? We'd like to hear about the years you've been away."

"We'd be pleased," said Karl, as Ingrid nodded in agreement.

Karl told about his double life as a student and an American intelligence agent. Ingrid listened eagerly, and the Lindstroms asked many questions about his years in Sweden and his new assignment in Washington.

As he and Ingrid were leaving, Karl said he hoped he would see them in church. "I'd like to introduce you to my wife, but I hope that won't cause you stress when you meet her, because Inge seems so much like Karla."

"You'll like her," said Ingrid. "She's from Sweden and is so friendly—and so pretty and talented!"

"Sounds as though we will want to add her to our family, as we already have with you, Karl," said Henrik.

Chapter 22: ASSIGNMENT WASHINGTON

Back in Washington, Inge glowed with happiness after meeting Karl's family and friends.

"We got back just in time, because I heard on the news that a blizzard hit Wisconsin just after we left," said Karl. "Good thing we left when we did!"

"Well, it feels cold enough here, without a storm," said Inge.

So they basked in the warmth of their apartment and in the warmth of memories of Karl's family and friends.

"I sure enjoyed seeing some of your earlier paintings," said Inge. "Now I think you and I both should start painting again. It might provide welcome relief from the intensity of our investigative work. Maybe we can arrange for an art exhibit like yours in Richland Center."

"Yup, time to start our search for Masonite," laughed Karl. "And if we can't salvage Masonite, we might have to actually buy some. But that would take away part of the joy of creating."

When they reported back for duty, the OSS assigned Inge the challenge of compiling information about the art likely taken by the Nazis. The OSS also wanted her to coordinate with the FBI unit specializing in art theft. So she slowly and steadily learned more about ownership of art in Europe, and she added that information to the evidence she and Karl had accumulated in Sweden.

Besides initially helping in the cryptography section of the OSS, Karl assisted in arranging a link to the French underground through his earlier contacts there. That responsibility expanded into greater involvement in the OSS counter-intelligence activity, including application of his graphics knowledge and skills to assist with the production of counterfeit money and documents for OSS agents who were starting to penetrate Europe.

Art Sleuths

Responding to the increasing demands of war, swarms of new residents poured into Washington to join the government bureaucracies. With restaurants and cultural events crowded, Karl and Inge turned to a new outlet for their limited free time—they started teaching an art history evening class at the Corcoran Gallery. As a bonus, they got the privilege of using a workshop in the gallery to produce their own art.

"Who knows," said Karl, "if we have some Jewish students, we might even get leads about Nazis stealing art."

No leads of that kind showed up, at least at first, but they did enjoy associating with the alert and informed "students."

Like so many teachers, Karl and Inge found that they themselves were learning about history from the students, as well as gaining new friends. And many of the students, who were also new to Washington, welcomed the chance to get acquainted with others with shared interests.

Gradually, both Karl and Inge began producing their own art again, and their efforts proved to be personally satisfying as well as interesting to their class. Soon several of the students asked to see the art.

The students reacted with surprise and keen interest as Karl showed his abstract designs with their architectural overtones. Of course, they enjoyed hearing about the scrounging by Karl and Inge for Masonite and other "art materials."

Inge's sculptural creations with tubes and cubes puzzled but pleased the students.

Before the end of the session, the students suggested that the class have an art show, including examples from anyone who wanted to exhibit, along with pieces from Karl and Inge.

At show time, families and friends gathered to look and wonder. The reception provided opportunity for questions and comments. A reviewer from the newspaper dropped in—thanks to an invitation from one of the students. And she turned the concept of art and community into an intriguing feature story.

Thanks to that publicity and word-of- mouth promotion, the class filled the room for the next session, with many returnees from the initial class.

Students identified guest speakers, and Karl and Inge invited them to share with the growing group.

By the spring of 1943, the OSS had built a strong foundation and linked effectively with the intelligence arms of the various military organizations and the FBI. As part of gaining effectiveness in infiltrating in Europe, the OSS started a campaign to add qualified intelligence specialists—"spies, to be blunt," the leaders admitted.

For Karl, that meant a new assignment as an OSS recruiter at military bases and at college campuses. So while Inge continued her work and fostered the popular art history course, Karl prepared for a countrywide program to enlist appropriate volunteers for espionage in Europe and the Soviet Union.

During his orientation, he learned that, though the Allies need the Soviet Union, the U.S. and Britain don't trust Soviet leaders—despite the many positive stories about the Soviet Union in the American liberal media.

Now, the OSS had just learned that Finland had intercepted the code used in Soviet intelligence activity, and the OSS desperately wanted that vital information.

Because of Karl's experience in the Scandinavian intelligence organization, the OSS asked Karl to postpone his recruiting junket and focus on getting that code—even traveling to Sweden and on to Finland if required.

Immediately, Karl re-activated his connection with Haaken and Kjell, and he learned that both knew about the Finnish copy of the Soviet code. But, getting a copy posed a challenge, because Kjell couldn't risk action from neutral Sweden. But the importance of the code, if a copy could be acquired, required a reliable, personal courier.

After much deliberation, Haaken sent a message back: "Kjell and I ruled out myself, too, because we can't risk corrupting the Allied intelligence organization here. So, my friend, that leaves you.

"We know that you might encounter considerable danger, though the Russians control Finland and are supposed to be our friends. After all, they're getting piles of military aid from the United States.

"We think we can tie you back into the art and architecture program at Lund University and set up a special interview about Finnish design at the university in Helsinki. Getting you in and out of Sweden complicates the venture, but several flyers of crippled British and American planes have successfully landed at Malmö instead of trying to return to England. You might sneak in there, too—with cooperation from Sweden.

"So, you could brush up on your flying skills in England, then borrow a British trainer and fly along the Oresund coast to Mälmo," said Haaken. "From there, you can go by train to Stockholm. Next you would take a ferry to Helsinki to a rendezvous with the underground in Finland.

"Then you would return to your façade of research at the Lund University while we set the schedule for the final leg of your flight. And that will pose another test of your skill and courage— flying back over the North Sea to take that precious code to England."

When Karl outlined the mission to Finland during a meeting at the OSS headquarters, he expressed his surprise at the importance of spying on the Soviets.

"We're committed to stopping Germany," said his supervisor in the meeting, "but we don't trust Uncle Joe much more than we trust Hitler. Demonic, both of them. Though we need Uncle Joe, we must watch our back. After all, it wasn't long ago that Russia signed a deal with Hitler, and then got stabbed in the back."

"I realize we'll be conducting a high-stakes mission," said Karl, "and this is one of the risks of war. Count me in—as if I had a choice," laughed Karl

"Sorry to be so blunt," said his supervisor, "but consider yourself expendable, like almost everyone else in this war. So we'll plan for the worst and hope for the best. Keep in mind that if the Russians even question your purpose, they'll shoot you down. And the German Luftwaffe would welcome a sitting duck."

At home, Inge cried when Karl explained his mission.

"The war has toughened me," she said, as tears flowed down her cheeks, "but even the slightest thought of losing you devastates me.

"Well," she admitted, "I did expect to miss you when you told me about recruiting for the OSS.

"I hope my work at cataloging art and handling our art class will keep me occupied, so maybe I won't have time to worry. I'm learning more and more about the use and potential of the information punch card to record our data, and I'm working with a team of keypunchers and readers."

"That sounds like our cryptography," said Karl, "and I only got a taste of it. So, now I can learn more from you.

"We do make such a wonderful team," he added, "and I'll certainly miss you while I'm gone, because we have shared so many projects and events. And physically," he added, as a hint for romantic sharing later.

"Umm, yes!" she answered.

After he caught a "hop" on a transport plane to the familiar Duxford airbase in England, Karl found the coordinator for his flight to Sweden.

"I hope this plane isn't much more complicated than a Piper Cub," said Karl to his American flight instructor, Lieutenant Jim Clark. "That's what I learned to fly. Hope a person never forgets how—like riding a bicycle," laughed Karl, with tenseness in his voice.

"This military Cub boasts more power and speed and flaps, but not much else," said the Jim, "so you should get the hang of it in no time. No retractable landing gear, of course. Not bright yellow, either. But an extra gas tank for an extended flight. It includes basic instruments, but no radio. But radio transmission would just alert a Messerschmitt anyway.

"So I'm ready when you are," he said.

In the air, Karl did soon feel comfortable—like riding a bicycle. The military model offered better vision, too. Landing proved to be a bit bumpy. Then he managed a takeoff—also a bit bumpy. But a few more tries by Karl reduced the jerkiness of taking off and landing.

"Good work," said the Jim. "You got back in the grove quickly! We'll practice more over the next few days, including some evasive maneuvers, such as sudden cut in air speed. Even an intentional stall. We'll review instrument readings to be sure you maintain altitude and don't get disoriented by fog or clouds."

Then they traced a route from Duxford across the eastern bulge of England.

"Remember, we are at 51 degrees longitude and right at the Greenwich line latitude. You'll be going toward Gothenburg, Sweden, to 58 degrees longitude and 12 degrees latitude. Before that, you must fly between Norway and Denmark, and hope you don't excite the Luftwaffe. Then you should be safe in Sweden as you fly south along the Swedish coast at 14 degrees latitude to Malmö at 55 degrees longitude, near the southern tip of Sweden.

"There you'll see a large airfield with a scattering of American and British bombers that couldn't make it back here after a bombing run.

"Your American colleague, Col. Haaken Hansen, and his Swedish associate, Major Kjell

Seastrand, await you for the rest of your mission. They'll help you with the next legs of your travel.

"For your return, you will reverse the route. Look for that eastern bump of England, and then look for the bombers and other aircraft here at Duxford—at the Greenwich line and 51 degrees longitude.

"We'll have your plane fueled and ready to go in the morning," concluded the Jim.

"Hope you don't need this parachute or life preserver," said Jim, in the morning, as he handed the gear to Karl. "So, cheerio, as they say here. Hope to see you soon," he added, as Karl revved up the engine, saluted and headed for Sweden.

Chapter 23: IN THE AIR AGAIN TO SWEDEN

Strange to be up here alone, over the ocean, thought Karl. *But I don't want company up here or down below right now. A Spitfire or Mustang would look mighty good when I return, though. I'm glad this military Cub with its plastic canopy provides good visibility up and around.*

Now I sense what Lindbergh experienced, even though I'm just a few miles from base and I'll soon reach my destination. Lindbergh probably moved along at a hundred miles an hour, too.

At least I don't see any threatening clouds ahead, just friendly puffy stuff. That might be welcome in case I have to play hide and seek from a

Messerschmitt. Sure wouldn't be a fair fight otherwise.

When he entered the friendly clouds, Karl watched the instruments carefully, to make sure he maintained a steady altitude and kept the plane on an even keel. And he checked his direction indicator to confirm he was on course.

Maybe I should thank the Russians, after all. They may be drawing Hitler's attention, so the Germans are less likely to notice me.

I'm getting groggy after only four hours. Time to take a sip of water—and think of Lindbergh's endurance.

That must be Norway ahead. Look at those mountains. Oh, they sure look good, but I must stick to the middle of the Skagerrak. I don't want any anti-aircraft potshots from Denmark or Norway. Sweden, you look beautiful, he thought, an hour later. *We're going downhill now! On to Malmö!*

He saw a welcoming committee as he taxied toward a hangar at the Malmö. *Hope you're there, Haaken and Kjell. I don't want my luck to change after the clear sailing here.*

After he shut down the Cub and climbed out— staggering a bit from sitting so long—he saw Haaken and Kjell walking briskly toward him.

"You guys look mighty good to me," he said, as they shook hands.

"The feeling is mutual," said Haaken, as Kjell slapped Karl on the back.

Then Karl looked beyond them and blinked in surprise. Anja and Jakob Lindfelt ran forward and hugged him. Behind them, Tore and Hanna hurried to greet him with big smiles.

"You look wonderful, Karl, even in that flying uniform!" exclaimed Hanna.

Tore shook hands, and then motioned all of them toward a room in the hangar. "We give thanks that you arrived safely, Karl, and we want to hear all about you and Inge in America."

In the meeting room, Haaken suggested they all sit down around the conference table "while I pour the coffee and hot chocolate and serve some pastries. We're eager for your report."

"If you don't mind, right now I'm eager to find a toilet," laughed Karl.

"Yes, you have been flying for a few hours," grinned Haaken.

"I'll show you the way," said Jakob.

On the way, Jakob declared: "I sure admire your courage and skill, Karl. Your life must be exciting!"

"Right now, too exciting," admitted Karl, "because I have to go to Finland and then scramble back to England."

As Karl sipped coffee and savored the pastries, Hanna immediately wondered about Inge and her life.

"She spills over with good health," said Karl, "and she radiates beauty. And she loves living in Washington."

"In what way?" asked a curious Anja.

"She feels gratified in compiling information about art for our secret service agency, and she's learning new ways to record data with special perforated card files so the information can be quickly accessible. We both teach an evening art history class for adults at an art gallery, and many of our students have become good friends. Besides teaching, we can use the gallery workshop to produce our own art."

"That does sound gratifying," agreed Hanna.

"I'll bet Inge has created some interesting sculpture," said Tore, with a smile.

"You should see her construction with cardboard tubes and cubes and other shapes. Her art is beautiful! And a reviewer from the newspaper wrote about our art, so now we have a full classroom of students.

"We haven't been able to weld art yet, though," smiled Karl. "Not part of the gallery workshop."

"Do you still use that panel board for your art, Karl?" asked Anja.

"Oh yes, Inge and I enjoy scrounging at construction sites, where we've collected a lot of Masonite scraps," said Karl. "My art still looks weird, but viewers—and reviewers—seem to appreciate it. Enough even to attract some buyers.

"Oh, I forgot," said Karl. "When we got to Washington, we arranged to drive to Wisconsin—using gasoline, not wood," he added, with a smile. "So now Inge feels she's a close part of my family, too."

"Your life sounds so good and we are so thankful," said Hanna. "And we love both of you so much!"

"You and Inge make us proud parents," said Tore, "and we admire the way you and Inge support each other and keep life interesting and fulfilling."

"Can we report at school about your life?" asked Jakob.

"About America and our life in our nation's capital," said Karl, "but not about our special work for the government. Remember the Swedish tiger."

"No, we don't want to give away any secrets," said Jakob.

"Can we brag about your success as artists?" asked Anja.

"Don't you have a Swedish tiger that keeps Swedes from bragging?" answered Karl, with a smile.

"Good answer!" said Tore.

"I hate to interrupt this stimulating conversation," said Haaken, "but let me explain the situation for Karl.

"First, we brought your family here, because we knew that traveling to them would not be possible. Next, you will have more time together at dinner tonight and breakfast in the morning, because you will continue to be together here in the hangar.

"Urgency prevails, Karl, so we will send you back to England just as soon as you complete the round trip to Finland with the precious documents you came for," said Haaken. "By the way, the Finns who will meet you at the ferry landing do speak Swedish—and so should you the whole time on the ferry."

"Hope my Swedish doesn't sound too American," said Karl, with a subdued laugh.

"Everyone else will just assume by your sound that you're from Skåne," smiled Haaken.

"We'll drop you off and pick you up at the train station. In Stockholm, another agent will take you to the ferry landing there…and he will stay with you the whole time," said Kjell.

"That makes me feel a bit more secure, so I won't screw up with all those connections," said Karl, with obvious relief.

"We understand, and deeply appreciate the risk you are taking," said Kjell. "Many leaders here and friends elsewhere, know of your skill and courage, and we hope and pray for your safe return."

When Karl and his agent-companion arrived in Helsinki, they went directly to the university for a previously scheduled meeting with the noted Finnish architect Alvar Aalto and some of his colleagues.

Despite the tension caused by the underlying reason for the trip, Karl relaxed during his conversation with Alvar and his associates. Not only was this the "cover" for his trip to Finland, it provided a personally enriching experience with the world-renown architect. In addition, he gained new insights about Germany when Alvar told about his association with the leaders of the German Bauhaus arts group. He explained that several of the Bauhaus artists had fled to America to escape Nazi persecution.

While at the university, one of Aalto's associates had quietly presented him with a bas relief wood sculpture, with the comment, "This is in special memory of Finland." Karl then understood that the carved piece contained the copy of the Russian code he had been sent to get.

Later, it served as a conversation piece with the wary Russian officials at the ferry check station, as they chatted about Finnish art.

Back in Sweden, all concerned breathed a sigh of relief—and declared their determination to complete the mission. So they wasted little time preparing for Karl's flight back to England.

At the airport, he saw another person in a flying suit who briefly puzzled him.

As he got closer, he suddenly heard an exclamation: "I'm so happy to see you again!"

"Jenny Henriksson! Can that be you?" exclaimed Karl.

"She's going with you, Karl. Let me explain," said Haaken.

"We found out she's a German spy, but also that she's fed up with the German atrocities she's been hearing about, in contrast to the peace she found in Sweden. So she's agreed to go with you to England and serve our cause," said Haaken.

"I don't blame you for skepticism," said Kjell, "but we investigated her situation every which way, and we feel she genuinely wants to help us against Hitler. Her real name is von Gruen, and she can be a tremendous help to the Allied secret service. We're willing to take a chance, so I hope you are, too."

"Well, Jenny, I enjoyed being with you at the University, so I expect to enjoy your company now," said Karl.

"By the way, do you know how to fly?" asked Karl.

"I've flown some, in a little plane like this," she said.

"Good! I got lucky coming, but by now your German friends may smell something fishy," continued Karl. "If we have to play hide and seek, your help in watching the skies and the instruments could be vital to our survival."

"You're fueled to the brim but you have a long way to go, so make it last," he said, with grim humor. "Remember that you have another parachute and life-preserver, which we hope you won't need," said Kjell. "Happy landing!"

As they cruised up the coast of Sweden toward Norway, where they planned to head west across the sea toward England, Jenny talked about the patriotism in her Prussian family. "But we all despise Hitler's vicious attack on the Jews! So, with despair about my country, I decided I can not contribute to that kind of atrocity, which is why I agreed to help the Allied secret service.

"Personally," she added, "I admire you and Inge. Now I am beginning to see your side of the war in a different way. Even Gerhart and Janna expressed their admiration for the two of you. I hope that some day we can all get together again."

As Karl looked at the clouds ahead, Jenny shouted, "Look up, to the left! A Messerschmitt!"

"Watch the instruments," said a tense Karl. "We'll head into the fog toward the Norwegian mountains."

Good thing they aren't the Rockies, or we couldn't clear them, thought Karl.

"We're up high enough but still covered by the clouds," said Jenny. "It looks like he lost us, but he won't give up."

"Now we need to get back on the course I wrote down on that pad," said Karl.

Just then they emerged in a clearing over a fjord.

"Here he comes again!" screamed Jenny.

"Hang on! I'm going to slow down and drop down," explained Karl, "and hope he doesn't have time to fire."

Then they heard an explosion. "He didn't make it. I hope we can," muttered Karl, as he struggled to keep the plane above the water and turned away from the wall of granite ahead of them."

"You did it, Karl!" shouted Jenny.

"We did it," corrected Karl. "Thanks, co-pilot.

"I think he was a Lone Ranger on the prowl," said Karl, "so let's follow this back to the ocean and head for England. And hope we don't have more company."

At the mouth of the fjord, Jenny advised Karl to ease west till they'd passed Norway and then angle southwest to England. She watched the direction indicator and suggested a slight correction.

They cruised steadily for nearly two hours, when Karl jolted their comfort: "I see a surfaced U-boat ahead. Their gun is turning toward us. Any clouds to hide in?"

"Off to the right," said Jenny.

"I'm going to zigzag in an irregular pattern so the gunner can't anticipate where we will turn, then hope and pray we can reach those clouds and we'll be out of range."

In the clouds, Karl expressed his relief: "Now they can't guess where we are, and we'll soon be out of range."

"Okay," said Jenny, "let's get back on track," as she indicated another course correction.

"How's our gas?" asked Karl. "Our evasions cost us a lot of fuel."

"How long to England?" asked Jenny.

"About two more hours," said Karl.

"We seem to be okay, but I hope we don't have to perform any more evasions," said a grim Jenny.

An hour later, Jenny shouted: "Two more planes! High to the left."

"Hot dog! Our guardian angels!" exclaimed Karl. "Those are American Mustangs that have come out to welcome us!"

"I'm mighty happy they showed up," said Jenny, "because they just chased off a couple of German planes.

"That was amazing, but we still seem to be on course," said Jenny. "Now what do we look for?"

"After we pass the eastern bump of England, watch for a small town and an airfield with a lineup of bombers and other planes," explained Karl.

"There go our Mustangs again," said Karl, "returning to the airfield and wagging their wings. Well, we can wag, too," said Karl, as he tilted their wings up and down.

"Aren't you feeling sassy," laughed Jenny. "And for good reason, I might add."

On the ground, Jim rushed to greet Karl and help him out so Karl could loosen up after the long flight. But the sight of Jenny in the plane startled him. "So you even picked up a passenger," he laughed. "Welcome back! Jolly good show, I must say.

"You must be important, because we have some brass from the Office for Strategic Services here to meet you," said Jim, motioning to the men walking quickly toward them.

After the brass identified themselves and praised Karl for his daring flight, Karl handed them a large package. "Here's your airmail delivery."

"A precious cargo," said one, "We thank you."

"Thanks also for delivering your important passenger," said another, as he helped Jenny out of the plane and let her stretch her legs, and led her away to the hanger.

"Everything go all right, Karl?" asked Jim.

"Well, we shook off a Messerschmitt and dodged a U-boat," said Karl. "Otherwise, smooth and steady. And my friend Jenny helped during the crunch times."

"Who is she, anyway?" asked Jim.

"A German spy. Friend or foe—I don't really know," said Karl.

Catching a "hop" back to America on a transport plane, Karl suffered through another long flight. But when Inge welcomed him home, their thoughts centered on a literal reunion.

"We can talk later," said Inge.

"Plenty of time for that," mumbled Karl, as he led Inge to their bedroom.

"Great reunion!" smiled Karl, as Inge prepared coffee the next morning.

"Couldn't have been better," agreed Inge.

"Now about my journey," said Karl.

"Let me report first that your family thrives and sends their love," said Karl.

"You saw them? How did that happen?" asked a startled Inge.

"Haaken and Kjell arranged for them to meet me at the Malmö airport, because I wouldn't have time to go to Helsingborg. They send their love, and they were delighted to learn about our happy and fulfilling life here," said Karl.

"We talked about their life now, as well as our growing roles in our government here. Jakob envies my life of adventure, but I reminded him that this trip was no joy ride. Anja got my permission to tell about our life in the capital of the United States. But I reminded her about the Swedish tiger, to keep silent about our spying. They enjoyed hearing about our art class and our art projects—and the newspaper review.

"Ready for another surprise?" asked Karl.

"I guess," said a cautious Inge.

"I brought a passenger to England—Jenny Henriksson," Karl announced.

"Jenny...the German spy!" exclaimed Inge.

"Evidently Haaken and Kjell convinced her to come over to our side, after her shock about Hitler's attack on the Jews.

"Oh, by the way, I did pick up the Russian code and deliver it to the OSS in England," Karl added, casually.

"Great work, my hero!" said Inge, as she hugged him.

"Did you enjoy smooth sailing all the way?" she asked.

"Not on the way back, because we had to dodge a Messerschmitt in a Norwegian fjord and run for cloud cover to avoid a German U-boat that fired at us. And the Mustangs that flew out to greet us drove off two more German planes as we approached England.

"Jenny proved to be a great co-pilot and helped us get back safely," said Karl.

"Thank you, Jenny," said Inge about the co-pilot. "I liked her before, and I like her even better now!"

Back in the OSS office in Washington, Karl received a commendation for his daring role in picking up the Russian code in Finland.

"Next, you will be recruiting for spies, starting in a special place called 'Little Norway' near Toronto in Canada, " said his supervisor.

"There, hundreds of 'escapees' from the German occupation in Norway eagerly await action, usually in some capacity with the Norwegian air force. We want to locate OSS candidates there, who could return to Norway to get information for us and to sabotage the German occupation. We will also want some to go elsewhere in Europe and even in Russia—primarily to collect information for us."

"Sending a Swede to Little Norway poses some risk," grinned Karl, "but this sounds like an ideal location for recruiting spies. What are the arrangements and when do I start?"

"We've alerted the commander of Little Norway about our needs and our plan of action, so you can start immediately. Now, because of our urgency and your flying experience, we're assigning a military Cub to you. That should impress those Norwegian airmen when you fly in. But guard your plane," smiled the supervisor. "We heard that they're an eager bunch!"

Karl surprised Inge in several ways when he announced the start of recruiting people to be spies: first, that he would go to the "Little Norway" flight training base in Canada; second, that he would fly a

Cub assigned to him; and third when he asked, "Would you like to join me when I practice with the Cub?"

"Sure!" she said, before she could even think about it. "That sounds a lot different than our last flight."

"Good," he said. "I've arranged with the OSS so we can start testing the Cub tomorrow, and I asked to train you as my co-pilot, like Jenny was."

"Sounds…challenging…frightening…and exciting," said Inge. "I hope I can get time off."

"Taken care of, through the OSS," said Karl.

"Maybe we can travel together in the future, like the Lindberghs flying together to places around the world," Karl added.

"You are a dreamer," laughed Inge.

"That's the American way," said Karl, with his laugh.

Inge caught on fast, as she assisted by checking the gauges while asking more about the venture.

Then Karl announced: "You're in control now."

"What?" she exclaimed.

"Just hold the stick firmly and watch this gauge to keep the plane level," said Karl, as he pointed to a gauge. "Watch this one so you maintain altitude, and this one for airspeed."

"My nerves can't take any more today," she later admitted, with relief, "so you're in control now."

Then Inge relaxed…and declared that "it was fun."

"Ready to land the plane?" asked Karl, with a grin.

"Not if you want to live to fly another day," laughed Inge.

"We'll go out again a couple of times for more practice—taking off and landing—before I leave at the end of the week," said Karl. "Then we'll do more when I get back.

"I'd take you along to Little Norway," smiled Karl, "but your beauty might cause a riot.

"Maybe we can fly together to Ohio and Wisconsin, on my next recruiting venture. We might find some German-Americans there who would be willing to help the OSS."

"Wonderful! I can hardly wait to see your family and friends again," said Inge.

Cruising along on a clear day, Karl enjoyed the beauty of the farms, mountains and forests as he headed for Little Norway. Before he reached Lake Ontario, he looked to his left to admire Lake Erie, and the view reminded him of his days as a sailor on the ore boats of the Great Lakes.

Then he got a quick glimpse of the spectacular Niagara Falls as he crossed Lake Ontario toward Toronto. With the Toronto baseball stadium as a landmark, he easily located the airfield next to Little Norway.

He surprised and pleased the Norwegians who met him, because he understood their language.

"You're Norwegian, too?" they asked.

"You may not like this," said Karl, "because I'm of Swedish descent. But I understand much of your language, though I can't speak your words very well."

"We don't speak English very well, either," said one of the Norwegians. "But I guess we'll make the best of it."

"So, we welcome you," said the other Norwegian. "And we have gathered many Norwegians who might help you. Some want to go to Norway to disrupt the Germans. Some others might be willing to infiltrate Germany or Denmark, where they could get by using the languages.

"Please come with us to our meeting room, where you can explain in more detail about the type of assignments you have in mind, how you might want to carry them out, and what kinds of risks might be involved."

In the room, Karl could understand much of the banter, but he planned to speak English. A translator would help him and the Norwegians.

He hardly needed to remind the group of the complications of the conflict, because most had already seen that in Norway. Karl explained the general purposes and organization of the American and British secret services, and then he added some specific ways the Norwegians could help. But he cautioned them about the great risk.

Several immediately wanted to go back to avenge Norway by gathering vital information for the OSS and causing whatever sabotage might be possible.

Others, less enthusiastically, offered to help as spies in other parts of Europe, though they admitted that their knowledge and language might limit their effectiveness.

Karl explained that they all would receive many days of training by the OSS, so they would be prepared as much as practical.

Art Sleuths

"You really hit the jackpot in Little Norway," said Karl's supervisor when Karl returned. "We'll adapt our training program to fit the Norwegians, and we will send a team of trainers immediately.

"Now, you certainly do have our approval to fly next to Ohio and Wisconsin, where you might hit another jackpot. Lots more German-Americans in the ROTC there. Even by flying there in our plane, you will make a strong impression of our capability.

"I heard that you didn't want to distract the Norwegians by taking Inge along there, but she should be an effective teammate in Ohio and Wisconsin. So get on with that as soon as possible.

"And, thanks again for the your great start at our recruiting."

"Wow! What beautiful mountains and forests!" exclaimed Inge, as they flew west over the Appalachians. "Flying at this altitude and speed provides a great view, and it helps me understand and appreciate the scope and diversity of America. Looks like flatland ahead," she commented, "and those green geometric shapes remind me of why the farmland attracted so many immigrants from Europe."

"A lot of them here came from Germany," explained Karl, "so that's why we decided to promote our cause at Ohio State University in Columbus. We might find some students who would be willing and able to infiltrate into Germany and get valuable information for the OSS. We'll connect with the ROTC first, but we've also arranged to meet with a few students majoring in art history. They might help us track down information about Nazi art theft operations."

"I sure could use some more support for that challenge," said Inge, "and I look forward to talking with those students."

"So do I," said Karl. "Hearing student reactions about the various ways of acquiring art—especially the Nazi way—should be interesting and revealing."

At a small airport near the university, the ROTC commander met them and expressed his eagerness to learn more about them. He explained, with a smile, that the small airport serves "our ROTC air force, because interest in flying has surged. So brace yourself for questions about your plane and your flight. We even include a smattering of women in our program, so they will bombard you with questions, Inge."

Karl and Inge did generate much interest and discussion with their presentation, and they even picked up some contacts to share with the OSS.

The women did respond enthusiastically to Inge. They praised her for her concern about the plundering of art by the Nazis, and she got some names to consider for future staffing.

Later, the select group of art students showed a stronger reaction about the art theft, and some indicated a possible willingness to serve the OSS as spies in Europe. As they eagerly questioned Karl and Inge about their background in art, the art students expressed their amazement that Karl and Inge had doctor's degrees and had exhibited and sold their own art. When the students heard about the art class at the Corcoran Gallery, several declared that if they were to ever live in Washington, they would like to enroll in that class as soon as possible.

Karl explained that next he and Inge would be flying to his school, the University of Wisconsin in Madison. One student mentioned his interest in architecture and wondered about Frank Lloyd Wright's impact in Wisconsin. That opened up another animated discussion.

After some refreshing sleep in the guest room at the ROTC hangar, Karl and Inge prepared for the final leg of their junket. They chatted with the ROTC crew that refueled the plane, who expressed hope that someday soon they might acquire a Piper Cub at least, since currently there was no plane at their little airport.

Before Karl and Inge took off, another member of the ROTC rushed out of the hangar to get their attention.

"We just got a tornado warning, so I thought I'd better alert you," he said. "The storm has passed beyond us and is veering south, so you should be safe. But tornadoes tend to be unpredictable, because they follow a random pattern and can unexpectedly turn and come back at you."

"I know," said Karl, "I've seen that happen in Wisconsin, but thanks for the warning. "

Up in the calm air, Inge wondered about tornadoes. "I heard about them in Minneapolis, but not in Sweden. First you scare me with blizzards and now with tornadoes. Folks here do have to cope with a lot of risks," added Inge.

"With our storms in the winter and summer, people do need to be scared—and prepared," said Karl. "Thank you!" said Karl as he reached back and patted a bundle behind them. "I feel a bit more secure because of these parachutes and life-preservers. But I sure wouldn't want to use a parachute in a tornado or a blizzard. Could get blown to Mexico."

"That looks like the Baltic Sea over there!" exclaimed Inge.

"That's Lake Michigan, and the sprawling city is Chicago. Not very many years ago, Chicago ranked as the second biggest Swedish city," smiled Karl.

"You mean, it had almost as many Swedes as Stockholm?" questioned Inge.

"Yup, hordes of Swedish immigrants poured in here, and then slowly moved west," said Karl. "Like Brooklyn, which had almost as many Norwegians as Oslo, for many years."

"Maybe you should try recruiting there," suggested Inge.

"Good thought," acknowledged Karl. "Worth a try, if we can focus on a gathering point like a university."

"Take a look there," said Karl, as he banked the Cub so Inge could see the city of Madison. "The university, along with the state capital, nestles on that isthmus between those two lakes."

"Must be beautiful," said Inge.

"Indeed it is," said Karl, "and you'll soon see for yourself.

"Now we'll head west and salute the folks at Taliesin.

"Down there, Taliesin—on the brow of a hill," said Karl, with tenseness in his voice.

"I hope we can take a closer look," said Inge.

"I'll alert them that we're coming," said Karl, as he wagged the wings in salute to a few persons, who waved in return. "Probably Mr. Wright waving at us," laughed Karl.

"Now, on to the tiny airport at Richland Center," said Karl. "I contacted Uncle Bill, so his family might be waiting for us. Ready for another family reunion?"

"I look forward to that with great pleasure," said Inge, as she squeezed Karl's arm.

"Well, I'll circle the town to let them know we've arrived, so they can get to the airport by the time we land," said Karl. "I'm thankful that wind sock is floating so calmly!"

"Tornado, stay away!" said Inge.

As the Cub dropped down, Inge exclaimed: "Look at that crowd. They must expect a big celebrity, not just the hometown hero," she added with a grin.

After they wheeled to a stop and Karl cut the engine, Bill and family rushed to meet them. Bill and Kirsten helped Inge out of the Cub and hugged her, while Eric and Ingrid went to the other side of the Cub to welcome Karl.

"Wow!" exclaimed Karl, "did you bring the rest of the town, too?"

"Most of it," laughed Bill.

"Get ready, both of you," said Kirsten, "because our newspaper and that Madison radio station want to feature you. I think a reporter from the Associated Press plans to send a story far and wide.

"George is here, and so are the Lindholms. They all think of you as part of the family, including you, Inge."

"Thank you," said Inge, as she brushed a tear off her cheek.

"We have the church all decked out to welcome you," said Ingrid. "We're so proud of both of you!"

At the church, Bengt and Tina met them at the door. "We got delayed a bit by a storm, so we didn't try to make it to the airport," said Bengt. "But we are so pleased and proud to have you back."

"Inge, you look so lovely in your flying gear," said Tina, as she hugged Inge. Then she turned to hug Karl, as Bengt wrapped his arms around Inge, and whispered, "Welcome home."

When Ingrid brought the Lindholms over, they too hugged Karl and Inge. "We're sure thankful to have you in our family," said Karin.

"Look who's here!" exclaimed Karl, as Andrew came with Anja and Dan in tow, and a blond boy held by Dan.

"Inge, meet my good friends, Anja and Dan Swanson," said Karl.

"And meet our son Steffan," said Anja, as Inge held his fingers.

"We're sorry we missed you the last time," said Dan. "You look great, Karl. And you look beautiful, Inge. Just like we expect of a Swedish flicka."

"According to the grapevine," said George, when he reached them, "you continue to create dramatic art, both of you. Of course, as your chief promoter, I've invited the news media, so be on guard," he laughed.

Art Sleuths

As the flash from a newspaper photographer's press camera cast shadows, the reporter asked about the art George had referred to.

"My first exhibit was right here," said Karl. "Now I team up with my wife Inge," said Karl as he drew her into the interview, "and we teach art in Washington, as well as creating our own art—each with a different style, of course."

In response to a question directed to her, Inge explained: "We met at the Lund University, where we each got a doctor's degree in art. Since then, we've had an occasional exhibit—in fact, the newspaper in Washington, D.C. reviewed our art favorably. And we've had many successful sales since then.

"As George will remember, my weird art tends to combine wild colors with architectural overlays," continued Karl.

"Do you still scrounge for Masonite panels as a substitute for canvas?" asked George.

"Oh yes, he does!" said Inge, with a smile and her Swedish sound, "We've visited the docks and construction sites, finding those panels."

"I even make them part of the art sometimes," explained Karl, "by using torn edges and dents and holes as elements of the design. Of course, I can also scrape and gouge, which you can't do on canvas. So you see why I call it weird," he laughed.

"Inge," asked the Associated Press writer, "do you paint that way also?"

"No, I lean toward industrial and graphic design," she explained, "so I combine tubes and boxes and other shapes in colorful assemblages.

"In fact, Karl and I met when we were both welding in the shop at the university," added Inge.

"When she raised her welding mask, I was overwhelmed by her beauty, as you can imagine," laughed Karl, as Inge's blush colored her fair skin.

"We're now involved in a gratifying teaching program at the Corcoran Gallery in Washington," said Inge. "We teach art history to a night class of adult students. They are a few of the thousands of new residents in the capital, so our class serves as a new supportive community for them—and for us. And we've discovered some outstanding artists through our class, too."

"I understand you both work for the Federal government," said the radio reporter. "How does your art expertise fit that?"

"First, I want to thank your station for helping me along early in my art career," said Karl, "because that caused a lot of interest...and surprise, because who would have thought of having a radio broadcast of an art exhibit!

"In Washington, we're both immersed in art for our government," as Karl answered the earlier question. "We're involved in trying to track the valuable paintings and other art taken during the war, mostly by the Germans from the Jews. When the Allies finish off this war, our leaders want to be ready to locate and return as much of this stolen art as possible—and punish those who stole it."

"We saw your dramatic arrival in your airplane," said the reporter. "Quite impressive, but for what purpose?"

"As part of our art research, we do need more experts," said Karl, "so we are recruiting at universities. At Ohio State, we enjoyed great discussions with art students, for instance, and we may be able to add some top talent to our staff.

"The Federal government lent us the plane, of course, for efficiency in our recruiting—and to make an impression of importance, you might say," smiled Karl.

"I was impressed," laughed the radio reporter.

Just then, Inge put her finger over her closed lips. "In Sweden, we have a tiger as a symbol on posters, which means silence—don't reveal too much information. That's like your American saying that 'loose lips sink ships!' So now that's a reminder that we can't say much more about our work in Washington."

"Welcome back!" came a greeting from behind the others.

"Ted Jamison! How great to see you again," said Karl.

"Meet my wife Inge, and Inge, this if my friend and roommate at Taliesin, Ted Jamison," said Karl.

"We flew over your place earlier today and wagged the wings," said Karl.

"So that was you," said a surprised Ted. "We sure enjoyed the salute."

"And I enjoyed our aerial view of Taliesin," said Inge, "with hope I could see it at ground level."

"That can be done," said Ted. "And here's the man who can arrange it. Meet Jason Stewart, who's responsible for the current repairs and improvements at Taliesin."

"Good to meet a Taliesin alumnus," said Jason. "We overheard the interview, and I'm greatly impressed by what both of you have accomplished. Your painting of architectural lines over splashes of color sounds intriguing, and I look forward to learning more about it."

"Here are two more for you to interview," said Karl, to divert the media folks. And they proceeded to ask about Taliesin.

The next morning, the family packed into two vehicles and drove to Taliesin, which only Bill and Karl had visited before. Taliesin thrilled Inge and the others with its placement, form and materials. Inside, they admired the simple geometric design of the furniture and fixtures in contrast to the textures of the rugs and wall hangings.

Before long, Karl and Inge returned to the Richland Center airport, and soon they were in the air again.

Flying past Taliesin, Karl again wagged the wings, as several persons below again waved.

Then they continued the short flight to the ROTC field at the edge of Madison. Their ROTC driver took them on a tour of the community and campus, as Inge exclaimed about the surrounding beauty. Before they went to meet the awaiting students, Karl pointed out the Lutheran Student Center. "My first home away from home," said Karl, "except for the ship on Lake Superior and Richland Center and Taliesin."

The current ROTC group does include several German-Americans, most from the Milwaukee area, and they expressed interest in serving the U.S. to counter the negative reaction to their German heritage.

With the art students, Karl and Inge enjoyed a stimulating discussion about art history, including the current turmoil related to the ownership of art. Inge noted a few students who might fit in her department.

"I'd like to see Minneapolis again, because we're so close, but we may already be overdue in Washington," said Inge. "Another time, I hope."

"That seems likely," smiled Karl, "with my roots in this area. So let's head for home as we know it now."

While they checked the plane before starting the engine, an ROTC student rushed out from the hangar. "We just got a warning about storm clouds," he said. "Probably part of the unpredictable weather after the tornado. This might blow over by the time you get close to South Bend, but you might want to take a look at our map that shows alternate airports, including some that are part of the ROTC system."

In the hangar, the three of them talked about the planned route.

"Unless you'd like to take a swim," said the student, with a smile, "you might not want to cross Lake Michigan during a storm. So you could swing around Chicago.

"If the storm looks bad immediately after you get up in the air, you could try to come back here. Or you could aim for our airfield in Rockford. We have ROTC at a small college there, and I'll alert them to be on standby."

Then he pointed out on the map other small cities with airports associated with the ROTC.

"In an emergency, you could go into a landing field in some of the smaller towns," he explained, "though you wouldn't have many support services available. And no ROTC to help you.

"Of course, if you have to, you could aim for a city park or ball field or even a pasture, just like another student from Wisconsin did when he flew an airmail route. Watch where you step in a pasture, though," he added, with a grin.

"Yeah, you mean Charles Lindbergh," laughed Karl. "My skill certainly doesn't match his. I might hit a cow, not just a cow-pie."

"This light-weight plane doesn't cope well in rough weather," said Karl, as he kept a grip on the stick and checked the gauge to keep the Cub on an even keel.

"That wonderful landscape ahead reminds me of a painting displayed at the university just before I left Madison," said Karl. "John Steuart Curry called his scene 'Wisconsin Landscape,' and it even shows storm clouds in a distance—like those ahead of us now."

"And I think of a Strindberg painting he called 'The Town,' with violent clouds hovering over a small community in Sweden," said Inge.

"He sure did show the power of nature in that," responded Karl.

"Somehow, my reactions—such as fear—crowd out my appreciation of art right now," said Inge, with a grim smile, "and I would vote to avoid that storm. I think the Cub might vote that way, too, by the way it's behaving."

"That makes the vote unanimous," said Karl, with his own grim smile. "Let's head for Rockford."

When they landed at the airstrip used by the ROTC, a student rushed toward them to direct the Cub toward the hangar. After Karl shut off the engine, he jumped down to help the student push the plane into the hangar.

"I'm Jorgen Hanson, and I'm glad to see you," said the student.

"And I'm more than glad to see you," said Inge, with a smile of relief.

"I'm Karl Nelson, and Inge is my wife," said Karl.

"We've heard about your tour of the area," said Jorgen. "While you wait out the storm, maybe you could speak to the students at the small college here. Rockford College only enrolls women, but it is associated with Beloit College in Wisconsin. So we operate this ROTC location for Beloit.

"When the student at Madison called, I hurried down from Beloit, about 20 miles away. I can fix up a place to bunk out here," said Jorgen. "And I can fix some lunch, if you don't mind a simple meal. But first I'll check with the Beloit and Rockford to see if we could set up a meeting this afternoon, if you're willing."

"Great opportunity," said Karl.

When Jorgen returned to the kitchen, he announced: "Done deal. I explained that you're recruiting for special Federal program related to tracking art missing because of the war. We expect a gathering of at least a hundred interested students."

"Good work," said Karl. "That makes me wonder whether you yourself would be interested in our art program, which could involve some spying in Europe."

"Probably so," said Jorgen, "because my draft board no doubt will be tapping me on the shoulder as soon as I finish college—or before."

"Okay, we'll get some of the needed information from you," said Karl, "and you'll hear from our Federal program."

During a lunch of sandwiches, fruit, milk and chocolate-chip cookies, Jorgen asked: "Are you both

Swedish? Inge, you sure seem Swedish, with your lovely sound and looks."

"Not a difficult guess," laughed Inge. "From Skåne and Lund University. Karl and I met there, though he's Swedish from Wisconsin."

"How about you?" asked Karl.

"Swedish-American," like you. "One of the thousands of Swedes from Rockford, including my girlfriend. Maybe some day I, or we, will get a chance to study in Sweden, like you did."

"Stay in touch," said Inge, with a warm smile. "Maybe we can help arrange that."

After they rode along with Jorgen to the Rockford College campus, Jorgen invited them to supper in the cafeteria.

"Actually, my girlfriend gets credit for this," said Jorgen. "She's president of the student body, so she also helped arrange for your presentation.

"Here she comes now," said Jorgen.

"Another Swedish beauty," said Karl.

"Swedish-American, like us," said Jorgen.

She hugged Jorgen, to his slight embarrassment, then introduced herself: "I'm Beth Sundskog, and I'm pleased to have you here and provide us insight into international relations."

"I'm Inge Lindfelt," she said as she shook hands with Beth, "and Karl Nelson is my husband and colleague."

After Karl and Beth shook hands, she suggested that they go through the cafeteria line and talk more as they eat dinner.

As she and Jorgen led the way, Beth asked Jorgen for information to use when she introduced Karl and Inge at the meeting.

"You'll be surprised to know that they each have a doctor's degree in art history from Lund University in Sweden. Karl also graduated from the University of Wisconsin and Cambridge in England."

"Wow!" Beth whispered back, "I am impressed, and I certainly will be honored to introduce them."

At the table, Karl joked with Jorgen about being surrounded by beautiful women. "How will we be able to concentrate on our food?"

"Good thing we've got two beautiful women right here at our table to keep our attention," laughed Jorgen.

During the presentation, Inge especially got attention from the 75 women in the gathering—as well as the 25 men. Faculty representatives from both colleges also joined the group.

Inge explained why she and Karl were visiting college campuses—to help staff a Federal program to gather and record information about valuable art from museums and private collections that might have fallen into the hands of the Nazis.

"We also want to know and record information about art that might have been acquired by Allied forces during the war, including the Soviets, even the British and Americans," added Inge.

One of the many questions came from a male student: "We heard from Jorgen that you came in your own plane. Are you in the air force?"

"We work for the Office of Strategic Services," explained Karl, "which provided my flight training, and now Inge is also learning to fly the Cub lent to us for this recruiting trip. But I—

we…are not very experienced, or daring in the face of a storm. So that's why we landed here instead of going on to South Bend."

"But we're glad for the detour," said Inge, "because we've enjoyed meeting with you and getting a sense of who you are."

Then Beth rose and declared: "We feel fortunate to have you visit our campus, and she led the loud applause from the group, including those from the faculty.

In private discussion later with students identified by Jorgen, Karl informed them that his role in the OSS also includes getting individuals who can work under cover in Europe to help locate the art thieves for future prosecution, as well as for the recovery of the art.

"This may not be the ideal campus for recruiting," he admitted, "because we particularly want Americans of German descent who might be able to infiltrate the Nazi organization and collect vital information. That calls for great skill and courage," he added, "but if you know of anyone here who seems to fit the requirement and wants to help, check with us later."

When Jorgen and Beth drove Karl and Inge back to the airfield, both said they would like to sign up for whatever appropriate way to serve.

Karl confirmed that the department would contact them. And he thanked both for arranging the meeting.

"We were surprised by the number of qualified students who expressed interest, so maybe you should be on our recruiting team," said Inge.

"See you in the morning," said Jorgen, after he checked on their sleeping arrangement.

"We'll be back to provide you breakfast," said Beth, as she shook hands with Karl and hugged Inge. "We'll miss you," she added quietly.

"I hope we'll see both of you in Washington," said Inge.

"Seems strange, all by ourselves in the big barn," said Karl later.

"Kinda spooky," said Inge, "but it's a lot better than challenging a thunder storm."

They pulled the single Army beds together and drifted off to sleep holding hands.

Suddenly, Karl woke. Then Inge did, too.

"I heard a noise that didn't sound like thunder," said Karl, as he reached in his flight bag to pull out a flashlight and his .45 automatic.

"I don't want someone messing with our plane, so when I get to the door, hit that switch to light the hangar," said Karl, as he went with Inge to locate the main switch.

When the bright light came on in the hangar, two men moving toward the plane stopped suddenly and looked like deer staring into headlights. Then they saw Karl with his automatic raised, and one shouted at the other to get out. Karl heard a metallic sound, as the men raced for the outside door and ran into the stormy darkness.

With Inge beside him, Karl checked the plane and the rest of the hangar.

"No sign of anyone else," said Karl. "But they left some tools behind," he added, as his flashlight revealed a scattering of a hammer, two screwdrivers, crow bar and an adjustable wrench. "That must be what I heard when they forced their way through the back door," said Karl. "I don't know what they were doing, but it wasn't just to get out in of the rain."

"One of them shouted in German to 'get out'," said Inge.

"Probably that German Bund organization that's headquartered near Chicago," said Karl. "Somehow they must have heard about our mission here, but they probably didn't expect this hangar to be occupied.

"That's the second time goons from the Bund have been out to get me."

"Second time?" questioned Inge. "What do you mean?"

"I was ambushed in the dark at the University of Wisconsin, when a campus leader didn't like me and sent his American Nazi thugs to teach me a lesson," explained Karl. "I survived, but the leader was kicked out of the university."

"Thankfully, you were prepared for this threat," said Inge. "Looked like you know how to use that weapon? Where did you learn that?"

"Part of my training by British Commandos," said Karl.

"And not from an Indian in Wisconsin," giggled Inge, as she squeezed his hand.

He laughed and said, "Let's block that door and then try to get some more sleep."

After the storm had moved on, the Cub purred smoothly to South Bend. At the airport, a student representative of Notre Dame picked them up for a drive through the pleasant small city and to the attractive campus.

Based on the OSS information he had received, the student explained that Notre Dame supports a strong education program for the Army Air Corps, and he said that particular group might be interested in the OSS.

That proved to be an accurate prediction, because Karl and Inge found many interested in the challenge of the OSS.

Even after warnings about risks of serving as part of the Allied counter-intelligence in Europe, both conventional and the military-connected students responded positively.

"Looks like we can head for home after our successful road-trip, so to speak," said Karl.

"We don't expect to travel elsewhere for now. The OSS leaders decided to focus on the northern middle states," he added, "ruling out students from the South, Northeast and West.

"The Southern drawl might cause a problem for a spy.

"And the OSS feels that many students from the Northeast might rather serve the Soviet Union than America, even though their family fortunes came from capitalism, not Communism.

"Flying to the West might challenge the endurance of the Cub as well as for us," laughed Karl, who realized the Cub would be inappropriate for that trip. "Anyway, the distance rules out the West for now."

"Too bad," said Inge. "I've enjoyed being your teammate, and I'm just getting the hang of flying."

"Well," responded Karl, "let's continue your flight training as often as we can. And we can stay on standby to fly to other assignments. For one thing, we have several museums to check out as part of our research. Maybe we'll check out art in Minneapolis after all."

Though the OSS leaders did suggest that Karl and Inge visit some other colleges, they expressed satisfaction with the current recruiting. Many of the college contacts, including Jorgen Hanson and Beth Sundskog, had signed up for the training related to recording art, and several had already started the training.

The leaders also thanked Karl and Inge for their connection with the French resistance, which has helped in North Africa and linked with the resistance in Italy for valuable support there.

Now they had learned that the OSS needs the help of the resistance organizations in western Europe, in anticipation of a huge Allied invasion there—once the Allied leaders settle their infighting, said the OSS leaders.

"We've stayed in touch with Jenny Henriksson—or von Gruen—so we can seek her help in Germany, as well as alerting the French, Dutch and Danish underground," said Karl.

"Jenny's motivation to help against Hitler just reached a new peak," said Inge, "because we learned that a member of her family was executed because of involvement in an assassination attempt on Hitler. A failed attempt, unfortunately."

"We can ask her to help us get in touch with our German friend from Lund University," said Karl. "According to Jenny, Gerhart Bayer and his wife Janna secretly switched allegiance to our side. He has connections with the labor organizations in Germany and the resistance in Poland, so he might take the lead in fostering espionage and sabotage at a critical time there."

Karl and Inge both offered to try to infiltrate the European resistance movement personally, but the OSS declared that Washington needs them within reach for their insights and interpretations about Europe.

That night, Karl and Inge reflected about the huge and complicated challenge for the Allies: War in every direction in Europe, bogged down by logistics and conflict in leadership; in the Pacific, the entrenchment by the Japanese at many locations, and the reality of the enormous distances across ocean posed no end of military problems.

After the June 7 massive Allied invasion of Western Europe, the OSS saw some hope for a foreseeable end of war there. But a desperation defense by the Nazis dashed the prospect of a quick end to the conflict, so the Allied forces slogged on, east and west.

Finally, with the end of that war in sight, the OSS chose to focus again on the Nazis' looting of art from many parts of Europe, to have a backup for the prosecution of the criminals. And to anticipate and possibly prevent the expected looting by the Soviet forces.

Earlier, Karl had suggested that the OSS investigating team visit American museums to get background about art in war-torn Europe. That turned to reality when the OSS eight months later decided to check those sources for information. Karl and Inge had already compiled information from the Corcoran Gallery, so their system for interviews provided a pattern for others.

While part of the investigative team went by train and car to museums in the East, Karl and Inge were assigned longer distances, again flying the military Cub. By this time, Inge had accumulated many hours piloting the plane, so she could share the flying time.

So they took off for another regional tour that included Pittsburgh, Cincinnati, Kansas City, Chicago—and Minneapolis.

They sought opinions and suggestions about art that might have been taken by the Nazis. Then they asked about what and how Nazis might have shipped and stored art in places such as Switzerland and South America.

When they reached Minneapolis, their reputation had preceded them, and the officials and students honored Inge as one the art academy's most famous—or notorious—students.

"Just think," said a female student, "an international spy got part of her training here."

Karl had alerted his family that he and Inge would be in Minneapolis. He explained that they would be staying at Fort Snelling, which currently houses the Federal military intelligence language school.

"Because of the OSS influence at the fort, we could host a family gathering there," said Karl.

"Great idea" said Bengt. "We'll alert the clan, so look for a bunch of us by midmorning on Saturday, and we'll bring the fixings for a picnic."

"The fort grounds will serve as a great place for a picnic," said Karl, "and it commands a magnificent view of where the Mississippi and Minnesota Rivers join."

"Wasn't that homecoming wonderful," exclaimed Inge as she revved up the Cub for the takeoff from the short landing strip at the fort.

"I look forward to the time my family can join with your family—in Wisconsin or Sweden," said Inge. "We'll blend so well and share so many interests."

Chapter 24:
NUREMBERG, GERMANY, THE YEAR 1945

When Germany surrendered on May 8, 1945, President Harry Truman declared the victory a tribute to the late President Franklin Roosevelt, who died on April 12.

Though the war against Japan continued, the Allied countries celebrated with a sense of relief and finality. But for the OSS, intense activity continued for compiling documentation about war crimes, in preparation for the trials to start in October.

Besides general counts of crime against humanity by the Nazi leaders, more specific charges included an array of atrocities that had been committed by Nazis.

Some of the accusations about atrocities did include widespread theft of valuable art. Though Karl and Inge and others involved in the investigation of the stolen art sensed the large scale of the plunder, they concentrated on specific data that might be useful in a trial.

The trial of the top Nazi officials at Nuremberg, Germany didn't require this information. But the OSS kept the information about the stolen art "in its hip pocket" as a possible aid to convictions of lower officials.

With Karl and Inge stationed in Nuremberg, the OSS felt ready to provide thorough and effective testimony about the patterns of the thefts and the subsequent concealment of art.

Though one court called them to testify, they felt frustrated because their information did seem nebulous. They knew the extent of the crimes, but direct connection of persons in the criminal events evaded them. Yet they resolved to continue pursuit of justice in whatever way possible in the future.

Because the courts didn't allow photography during the trials, Karl and Inge began sketching the scenes and primary individuals, using charcoal and colored pencils—each in a different style. When a foreign correspondent for the Associated Press happened to see and admire their art, he asked about purchasing the right to copy them to send them via wire-photo. So, with the okay of the OSS, they continued to sketch during their time on standby.

After they explained to the prison officials that they had met Albert Speer and would like to talk with him again, they finally got permission, based on their OSS credentials, to visit Speer.

With a little prompting, Speer remembered Karl's interest in architecture and the art study pursued by both of them. In carefully couched terms, he acknowledged that the siren song of power tempts many, including himself.

Karl and Inge learned later that Speer accepted blame without trying to excuse his collaboration with Hitler.

Before long, one of "Murrow's Boys"—the radio reporters working with Edward R. Murrow to provide news of Europe to America—also discovered them. First, he asked about their art, and that led to questions about their reasons for being at the trials. They carefully and cautiously told about their investigations about the theft of art during the war.

During the interview, Karl laughed about the past repeating itself, as he told about how a radio review of his display of art had generated interest in that exhibit. Of course, as a radio reporter, the "Murrow Boy" turned that into part of his human-interest broadcast about Karl and Inge.

Before long, Karl and Inge reached the status of minor international celebrities, with added attention because of their brief talk with Speer. Gradually, their modest fame proved to be valuable in generating more leads about art stolen by thieves from several countries.

They also got inquiries related to their future careers, as they heard from museums, publishers, and universities. So they began to think seriously about their future, and slowly they acknowledged that they wanted to continue as art detectives, while developing as artists themselves.

They also admitted to themselves that exposing crime, even if it involved gifts or sales to noted museums, could be a risky commitment. But exciting and gratifying, they concluded.

Despite their new popularity, they still experienced blocks of free time from the courtrooms and interviews. So, as soon as possible, they checked in at the nearby Army air base, where they explained that they needed to fly a certain number of hours to maintain their military pilot status. Meanwhile, the OSS wanted them to investigate Sweden's accumulation of American planes that had been "ditched" at an airfield near Malmö.

Before long, they were back in the familiar military version of a Cub.

When they flew to Malmö, they ran into a pleasant surprise—Kjell Seastrand. He explained that he supervises the handling of the "captured" Allied aircraft, and he shared a wide range of stories about his current assignment. Some "emergency landings" in Sweden, he explained, resulted from convenience and choice, and many of the "captured" aviators found a wife in Sweden and settled down to stay. Also, Sweden recycled several of the "captured" bombers to serve in its new international airline flights.

Before they left, he invited them to meet his family. During the dinner, Kjell summarized the sequence of his activities, and he complimented them on their continuing commitment to investigation about art.

When asked about Haaken, Kjell became subdued as he reported about Haaken's death. He explained that Haaken had volunteered to infiltrate the underground activities in Germany. Your Lund schoolmate Gerhart Bayer might be able to provide details, because he teamed up with Haaken in several underground ventures.

"By the way," said Kjell, "Hans—at Dolman Paper Company—has asked about you two several times, and he added that your friends at the Dolman mill have expressed their concern and interest. Of course, by now, many have read about your life in the spotlight."

Kjell also told about the fear and then relief shown by the people of Norway. "My intelligence counterpart in Norway explained that Hitler's 'Final Solution' of exterminating the enemy kept all of Norway on edge. Fortunately, many top leaders of Germany managed to intervene to prevent such diabolical action.

"I learned also that the Nazis grabbed art in Norway and hid it or sent it elsewhere," added Kjell. "So you might want add Norway to your list of places to investigate."

"Well, Inge, we might as well put our flying time to good use, so let's drop in on the family," said Karl, with a grin.

"Your relatives first," said Inge. "I recall that Tomelilla has a small golf course, and we could land there."

"Okay," said Karl, as he headed for a phone. "I'll call a family conference and hope a few will meet us."

By mid-day when they arrived in Tomelilla, much of the town as well as Karl's relatives waited for the Cub to land. Karl's family proudly introduced the others to their honored relatives, and then they all went to the community center for lively conversation during an improvised smörgåsbord.

"Now I feel like I should take a nap," said Karl, as he patted his full stomach. "But we must march on. Does your family know we're heading their way?"

"They're probably arranging a smörgåsbord right now," laughed Inge.

"Okay, Madame Pilot, off we go into the wild blue yonder," sang Karl.

Back at Nuremberg, they reunited with more friends from the past. Gerhart, Janna and Jenny contacted them and expressed great interest in getting together.

"For some time, we wondered about such a possibility," said Gerhart, "and then, suddenly, the two of you appeared in the news. And what great stories you shared!"

"We live in an old mansion commandeered by the OSS," said Karl, "so come on by and enjoy a taste of luxury. You probably haven't savored excellent food for a while."

"You're right on that," said Gerhart, "so we'll gratefully take you up on that offer. And more important, we want to know more about the amazing life you and Inge are leading."

When their friends arrived, Karl was surprised to see four. Gerhart smiled when he saw Karl's reaction: "We thought you might like some American company, so we brought Fredrick Karlstrom along. Actually, as you can see, it's Army Lieutenant Karlstrom."

"Actually, it's Fred," he said, as he reached out to shake hands. "Gerhart assured me we would have a lot in common, starting with our Swedish heritage. And I was curious to meet someone who has been in the news so much."

Karl welcomed them in, as Jenny hugged him. "Actually, I brought Fred. And we met because of our Swedishness," she laughed.

Then Karl shook hands with Janna: "Another rising artist, I understand. We remember well how you helped connect us with publishers in Germany."

When Inge came out of the kitchen, the reacquainting and the introductions started over. "We'll soon have some food," she said, "so sit down and enjoy our luxurious borrowed living room, before we move to our ornate dining table. I guess we need to thank a countess or some other aristocrat for our quarters."

"I left something outside the door," said Gerhart.

When he came back in with two large bottles, Janna explained: "Gerhart knows this brewmaster and particularly likes the beer he makes. So he had to bring some to share."

"Maybe he doesn't want to admit it until you taste the beer," said Jenny, "but Gerhart actually is the mysterious brewmaster. And we give his brew top rating."

"A good, practical hobby," admitted Gerhart, "especially when almost everyone in Germany scrapes by. My 'home brew' proves to be popular."

During dinner, the conversation jumped around, as everyone seemed to have questions at the same time.

"Inge, I guess that you are from Skåne, by your beautiful sound—and looks," said Fred.

"How does an Amercan, who doesn't sound at all Swedish, know that?" asked Inge.

"Two of my grandparents were from there and the other two were from near Linköping," explained Fred. "Even as kids growing up in Minnesota, we could tell the difference when we heard them talk— in Swenglish, of course."

"What is 'Swenglish'?" asked Janna.

"That's what the Swedish immigrants spoke in America—neither Swedish nor English, but a mix that was often humorous," answered Fred.

"You said you noticed Jenny's Swedish sound," commented Inge.

"I went to see an art exhibit on the base and I overheard this English Germish, you might call it. So I had to find out the source of this familiar but different sound."

"Of course, in American style, you introduced yourself," laughed Inge.

"Sure, and then she introduced me to Janna and Gerhart," said Fred. "I learned that all three were exhibiting art that day. I immediately liked them and their art."

"Sounds a bit like the way you two met, as I recall," said Jenny.

"A bright day in my life," said Karl. "We were both welding in the art department shop. When I glanced toward Inge, the light from her welding caught my attention. Then she dazzled me when she flipped up her welding mask."

"And, guess what, Fred! This American," said Inge, as she touched Karl's arm, "immediately invited me to lunch."

"Well, I was new at the University, and I wanted some help learning my way around," said Karl.

"Fred, you'll recognize this—from my time in Minneapolis, I called it a 'pick up'," said Inge.

"The American way!" said Fred. "Good going, Karl! Congratulations on your wonderful pick up!"

Eventually, Karl asked Fred about his assignment in the Army,

"I'm in an engineering unit," explained Fred, "and we're trying to patch up the damage we caused. Right now, we are literally patching—enough so Germany can sort-of function."

"What part of Minnesota are you from?" asked Inge.

"Mankato, south of the Twin Cities," said Fred.

"I visited there when I was at the Art Academy in Minneapolis," said Inge. "A beautiful city, like Minneapolis."

"I dealt with more of the grubby part," said Fred. "My dad has a gas station and garage. And we did construction work, too—anything to survive the hard times. Like you two, I did some welding, along with all kinds of other repair. That led me to the University of Minnesota to study engineering."

"From your radio interviews, Karl, I understand that you studied architecture as well as art," said Fred.

"At your rival, the University of Wisconsin," said Karl.

"Not much of a rivalry recently," boasted Fred, "considering our Gophers beat your Badgers."

"Did you play for the Gophers?" asked Karl.

"Nope. High school football was more than enough for me," admitted Fred. "Besides, I had to study hard after coming out of what was called a trade school. Still, what I learned at that trade school sure helps me now."

"I know what you mean," responded Karl. "I worked on ships and docks at Duluth, and even that adds reality in architecture for me."

"Let's do this more often," said Inge, as the guests were leaving.

"I could get used to this luxury," said Janna, "but you might enjoy the simplicity of our flat. Gerhart gained an appreciation for contemporary Scandinavian design while he was in Sweden. And he's made some of our furniture."

"And brew beer too. I'm impressed," said Karl. "And I would like to see your furniture—and taste your beer."

"So would I," said Fred."Making furniture appeals to me. Well, in case you need to use power woodworking equipment, we do have almost everything at the base. Welding, too," he said as he smiled at Karl and Inge. "I'm sure I could arrange for you to use the shop in the evening. And we could enjoy working together."

"I'll take you up on that, to make my own frames," said Janna. "They're scarce and expensive."

"I'm with you, Janna," said Jenny. "We could start a business making frames for others, too."

"What a treat that was," said Inge, as she and Karl washed the dishes. "I look forward to being with them again. And I might like to do some woodwork, too. Maybe even weld again."

"What an interesting and refreshing change that would be from the constant stress of our investigations," said Karl.

Chapter 25: WASHINGTON, D.C., THE YEAR 1948

The OSS encouraged the media attention about the investigative crusade led by Karl and Inge. As a result, museums, universities and families began contacting them.

Museums and universities with big art collections expressed concern for their reputations, as the stories about art stolen by the Nazis spilled over into scrutiny of other questionable sources of art. Already, the FBI tracked art donated with exaggerated claims for income tax deductions. Galleries involved in buying and selling art sought advice from Karl and Inge, as they worried about the influx of work by skilled forgers.

So, with the war crimes trials winding down, Karl and Inge realized how much they had benefited from the extensive publicity about their own background in art as well as their investigative successes.

"Time for us to set up shop and capitalize on the momentum," said Karl, as he and Inge pondered their future.

As a first step in testing the water and learning the territory, they signed up for a speaking tour of the United States. By incorporating anecdotes from their investigations, lecturing about art in a knowledgeable way and displaying their own art, they soon became the stars of the lecture circuit.

Their own art generated great interest and dramatic sales, so they had to replenish their supply steadily, while trying to maintain the integrity of their creations.

They also encountered enemies, such as American organized-crime syndicates that consider art a high-stakes commodity to acquire for wheeling and dealing.

When inquiries from the Mafia turned to threats, they connected with the FBI art-theft unit for advice and protection. And the FBI welcomed joining forces with the acclaimed art experts, so they all could share expertise.

In the newly formed United Nations, the probing for "lost art" continued, and the art-search section also sought the famous art duo to advise and assist.

Both the FBI and the UN encouraged them to promote the interest in missing art by continuing to lecture and participate in appropriate events. "We'll be in the shadows," they assured Karl and Inge.

The UN funded a special investigative junket by Karl and Inge to Norway. The UN sponsors assured them that the idea of the visit did not arise because the UN Secretary General is a Norwegian.

"But that might help us anyway," said Karl, "because our Swedish connection might cause some animosity otherwise."

Finally, they felt, they might have a chance to contact the Norwegian relatives of Haaken Hansen and tell about Haaken's heroics and his untimely death. Earlier, they had tracked down his family in Wisconsin, and they told the story of his secret life dedicated to the security of the United States and its wartime allies.

In Norway, the extent of the massive German fortifications along the coast shocked them, not only by the complexity of the system but also by the enormous extent of work and materials required.

"The work," explained their Norwegian guide, "came largely from Norwegian and Russian prisoners, and Germans forced the Norwegians to provide support in the form of food as well as material needed to pour the tons of concrete for the bunkers."

At Karmøy, a ferry-ride from Stavanger, Karl and Inge saw the kind of rocky terrain that must have challenged construction, but also provided ideal vantage points for the Germans.

While there, a former member of the Norwegian underground, who had heard about their search for stolen art, shared a story that some type of sculpture or jewelry had been hidden in the concrete of the bunker they visited, and he wondered about the chances of locating and retrieving it.

Karl noted the information, and he mentioned that the continuing refinement of radar and sonar might help in a search some day. "Otherwise," he added, "it would be worse than looking for a needle in a haystack. At least in a haystack, a simple magnet might help."

While in Norway, Karl told about his visit to "Little Norway" in Canada. Suddenly, a man in one audience stood up and shouted, "I was there!" So Karl thanked him and the thousands of other Norwegians in Canada who flew bombers and participated in espionage and sabotage against the Axis.

In Oslo, they met with a large contingent of Haaken's relatives, eager to hear about his dangerous life and his heroic death.

Karl and Inge both expressed the importance of their friendship with Haaken, as well as their great appreciation for his skillful coordination of their own counter-intelligence activities out of Sweden.

From Norway, they headed for Helsingborg to see Inge's family.

"For once," Inge announced to her mother, "we're not in a hurry. So I hope you can put up with a couple of loafers for a few days.

"We want to look around for a plot of land here, so we could live in both countries," said Inge. "Then we could all share. We are so sorry that we missed so much here because of our duties. But we are thankful for Anja and Jacob and their families, though we regret missing graduations, weddings and baptisms."

"And we're hoping you will add to our wonderful grandchildren," said Hanna.

"We hope so, too," said Inge. "We certainly enjoy the trying," Inge laughed, and so did Hanna.

"But now, more and more, Karl and I need to go separate ways to take care of our extensive commitments," explained Inge. "And we feel we should pursue individual identities, after being so continually linked, even though we treasure that sharing. Now I need to expand my own expression in art, and so does he."

"I understand that," said Hanna, "with your talent and education and experience. But Tore and I both worry about the risks associated with your flying, your fame and possibly your financial challenge. We're certainly able to help you with money, if you need that."

"No, don't worry about that," said Inge. "We can talk all about that at dinner, when Karl and Dad come back from the plant."

During dinner, Karl laughed that on this trip they missed driving the wood-burning Volvo, and the military Cub as well. "But the train felt relaxing."

Like Hanna's concern before, Tore wondered about the stress in their life.

"Excitement might be the better word," said Karl, "but we do welcome some Swedish calm."

"Karl, Mom said she worries that we may be stressed because of finances."

"I do wonder, also," said Tore, "and you can count on us for support."

"Actually, we do have money worries," said Karl, as Inge looked puzzled.

"I can imagine that," said Tore.

"Well," said Karl, "our financial worries come from handling our amazing income. Who would have guessed that a couple of young artists could be millionaires."

"You earned that from art!" exclaimed a surprised Tore, as Hanna looked just as surprised.

"Let me share our basic earnings pattern," said Inge. "We're paid to consult about art collections for a variety of clients. Law firms also pay us for our expertise. Our lectures also pay well. So do our newspaper columns and radio broadcasts about art, and a movie company and a television station might soon feature us. Magazines and advertising agencies pay us well for our designs, and we earn thousands by selling our own art, thanks to all the publicity about us."

"Sounds like you're a well-oiled machine," said Tore. "Maybe you can lend us money," he laughed.

"How do you manage your income when you keep so busy?" asked Hanna.

"We delegate much of that responsibility to our expanding staff and to a good accounting firm, which, by the way, keeps a tight rein on our spending," laughed Karl.

"But we did get a plane for our 'business'—a surplus military D-17S Beechcraft lent to us by the CIA, so we can respond quickly when needed," said Karl. "It certainly boasts much more power, range, speed and maneuverability than the Cubs we flew before. And the military mechanics souped up the engine and took great pride in adding the latest refinements, such as better controls, retractable landing gear and landing lights "

"Many other flyers consider our bi-plane obsolete," added Inge, "but then we impress them with the way our Staggerwing performs. The positioning of the wings provides us with good visibility. Besides, we like the distinctive look of our antique with its Swedish colors of yellow wings and blue fuselage. It's a work of art!"

"Its reduced stall speed saved us in one recent 'dogfight' when a Mafia plane tried to shoot us down over Lake Michigan," said Karl. "Dogged by danger," laughed Karl, as Inge groaned.

"We're still on call by the CIA for art investigation and testimony," he explained, "so the CIA arranges for the gas and maintenance and provides hangar space at our local airport," added Karl.

"I must say, art sure has taken on a new dimension in my mind," said Tore.

"But I still wonder—just where do you live now, anyway?" asked Hanna.

Chapter 26: SWEDESBORO, NEW JERSEY, THE YEAR 1950

"Down on the farm," chuckled Inge. "Come and see us at our beautiful place in New Jersey. When we found a piece of land near Swedesboro, in the heart of the New Sweden settlement in America, we couldn't resist. We can even attend the Old Swedes church there. And we can easily get to New York, Philadelphia, Wilmington and Washington.

"Karl designed our dramatic buildings, with some help from his friends at Taliesin. We'll send you a copy of a magazine story about our farm, to entice you to visit.

"Now, for our business called Svensk-art, we're also building an art studio, gift store and workshop, complete with a furnace so we can blow glass. And we can weld, of course," she added, with a chuckle.

"I'll send you a copy of another magazine article about our art compound, to lure you," she grinned.

"Here's an enticement for Jacob," added Karl. "Remember the book *Last of the Mohicans* I sent to him, with those great illustrations by N.C. Wyeth. The library in Wilmington includes a display of many of Wyeth's action paintings, and that's just across the Delaware River from us. I always enjoy seeing them."

"So do I!" interjected Inge, "And I'm sure Jacob would find them impressive...as all of you would."

Later, Inge reflected about their interesting life: "Fame does produce amazing rewards."

"And risks," admitted Karl. "Crime organizations, ethnic groups and even some governments and museums threaten us periodically for our past and present investigations of art with questionable ownership. Coordinating with the FBI offers some sense of security. And so do the .45's assigned to us by the CIA."

Before Tore and Hanna went to sleep that night, he whispered: "Who would have thought art could be so lucrative," said Tore.

"And so risky," said Hanna.

Back in New Sweden, Karl and Inge devoted the next few years to completing the first stages of their art community, with little interruption to serve the needs of the CIA and the FBI.

Besides traveling to Princeton University and other nearby locations to deliver lectures and make presentations and participate in interviews, they started preparations for a book of their own art to be sold in their shop and at other outlets.

In Philadelphia, Curtis Publishing had increased involvement in book production, partly to offset the decline in their traditional magazine publishing. So Karl and Inge arranged to visit the legendary company.

During their visit to the Curtis headquarters, they both basked in the gallery of paintings by Norman Rockwell and other illustrators who contributed to the popularity of the magazines published for many years by Curtis.

Before they left to go back to Swedesboro, they received an assortment of high-quality books and prints as examples of Curtis printing for Karl and Inge to consider in planning their own book— and to consider for selling Curtis books in the Swedesboro shop.

Weeks went by before Karl and Inge found time in their hectic schedule to peruse the books and to think about what they might include in a similar book.

As they slowly paged through one exquisitely printed book, Karl stopped in the middle of turning a page. "Hold on, let me back up," he said, with a sense of excitement. "I just saw a ghost from the past!"

When he got back to the "ghost" painting, Inge added her excitement: "That's one of the missing paintings we searched for right after the war!"

"And we never uncovered a hint of its location!" exclaimed Karl. "So how could it be reproduced here?"

"I don't recall any sign of it in all the information we compiled on those thousands of IBM punch cards, but we might start searching that CIA file," said Inge, as she thought back about the massive indexing project.

"I hope they've put that information on a computer by now," said Karl, "but, sorry to say, after all these years, the art may not rate a very high priority."

"Let's give it a shot anyway," said Inge. "Maybe all our skill and study of art will finally help solve a mystery—and a crime!"

Though primitive, the CIA computers had converted the information from the cards and had added reproductions of many of the paintings in question after the war. So, led by Inge, a team of CIA experts searched for the mysterious painting. Though the well-known missing painting surfaced as an entry, the computers provided no additional information about its current existence.

The search got the attention of others in the CIA, but they admitted the CIA had shifted priorities to current international urgencies. So they recommended involvement of the FBI art-theft unit.

Meeting with the FBI agents, Karl and Inge learned that the Mafia now used many tactics to launder their crime-related money into legitimate businesses—such as selling expensive art reproductions.

As the agents heard more about the role of Karl and Inge in tracing stolen art after the war, the FBI team picked up enthusiasm for the current twist in laundering.

"Maybe we can actually nail some of their honchos for major theft, not just for our standard charge of income-tax evasion," laughed the FBI leader, in anticipation of fresh success.

"Time for a working vacation," Karl announced several days later. "Let's get out of town while the FBI takes over."

"Sounds good to me!" said Inge. "What do you have in mind?"

"Our friends from Taliesin have encouraged us to visit Fallingwater, so this might be a perfect time for a drive in the Pennsylvania mountains," responded Karl. "Should be wonderful fall foliage. Those winding roads will make a good test for our vintage Volvo—but this time not a wood-burner!"

"You've talked me into it!" laughed Inge. "Another special honeymoon!"

"I sure remember the first one," smiled Karl. "In a mill town in Sweden. Now we can make love in Mill Run, Pennsylvania!"

On the road two weeks later after making arrangements for their departure from the farm, studio and shop, they started west.

"Goodbye city! Hello country!" shouted Karl, as they left the Philadelphia area and connected with the Pennsylvania Turnpike.

Many miles and a few tolls later, they turned off to Donegal on Route 31.

"Now we're actually heading for the country," said Karl, as they entered the twisting road toward Fallingwater.

But a few minutes later, Inge screamed: "Look out! No! That truck might hit us!"

"Hang on!" shouted Karl, as the truck crashed against the Volvo and pushed it off the road and down a steep embankment.

First the Volvo slid, then hit a rocky outcropping and rolled over and over till it landed on its wheels against rocks and trees.

Stunned after being jerked and bounced down the steep and rocky slope, Karl and Inge, with blood running down from their battered heads, sat covered with pieces of glass under a caved-in roof.

Slowly gaining consciousness, Karl wiped blood from one eye and looked with shock at Inge.

"Let's try to...get out of the car...up the hill," stuttered Karl, "or no one...will find us."

When he tried to move, he realized the seat belt held him. So he unbuckled the belt, with subconscious thanks to God.

His door refused to open, so he climbed out as carefully as possible through the broken window. Then he staggered to Inge's side of the car.

"Open! Dammit!" he shouted, as he pulled her door loose.

He held Inge in place and unbuckled her seatbelt, as she moaned from the pain. Then he gradually eased her out of the Volvo.

After trying to carry her up the rugged slope, he realized he would have to go up alone to try to get help.

"It hurts," she mumbled, as he covered her with his bloody jacket.

Slowly, he crawled and stumbled up the slope. At the top, he flopped down at the roadside, limply raising his hand when he heard a vehicle approaching.

A yellow power-company truck screeched to a stop, narrowly missing Karl at the edge of the road.

As the driver climbed out of the truck, his partner grabbed the truck radio. First, he cursed at the static, but then got a response, so he reported the emergency.

"My wife! My wife!" groaned Karl, as he pointed down the hill.

"Help's coming," said the driver, "but I'll go down and check. We may have to leave her there till the ambulance gets here."

"Suppose so," stammered Karl. "I pray she's okay."

When the highway patrolman arrived, he checked Karl and looked down the mountain. "Looks impossible to survive," he quietly commented to the truck driver.

Then the ambulance arrived, and one attendant administered aid to Karl, while the patrolman and truck driver went with the other attendant down to the car.

Slowly and carefully, they carried the semi-conscious Inge up on a stretcher. In a short time, the ambulance headed for the Donegal hospital with her and Karl.

"Can't believe they got out alive!" said the patrolman, as he and the two from the truck examined the area.

"Looks like they skidded sideways off the road when another vehicle hit them," said the patrolman, as he examined the marks on the road and paced off the length and width of the skid.

When another patrolman arrived, he photographed the road and the sideways slide of the car down the mountainside. "Something mighty fishy here," he declared. "Looks like the driver's side was pushed in—and not just from rolling over down the rough terrain. Strange coincidence that this short, straight section doesn't have a guard rail like the curve just ahead."

As he photographed the wrecked Volvo, he noticed the seat belts. "Those safety belts must have saved them. And a miracle that the roof didn't cave in more. They're mighty lucky to be alive!

"Guess we can report in," he added. "That car won't be going anywhere. Be mighty tough to get it back up to the highway, too."

In the hospital emergency room, the doctor on duty examined Inge and Karl. He and the attending nurse administered superficial treatment and provided relief from pain. Then he recommended that both be taken to Pittsburgh for more intensive care, and he alerted the hospital and arranged for an ambulance.

But a startled patrolman stopped the action. "I just called the emergency number in the man's wallet, and I got the CIA in Washington. The CIA will immediately dispatch a medical helicopter to transport them to Bethesda.

"Obviously, we're treating some important folks here. A lot more than meets the eye.

"While you get them ready to travel, I'll get ready to help the CIA investigate this strange incident.

"First, I'll call another number in his wallet—a manager of a business called Svensk-art in Swedesboro."

At Svensk-art, the manager alerted the staff about the injuries from the traffic collision and explained that a CIA helicopter will bring Karl and Inge to a hospital in Washington. "For now, we won't respond to any inquiries until we hear from the CIA. Evidently, the CIA suspects a link to investigations about stolen art.

"I'll contact the Taliesin host at Fallingwater and explain as much as I can about the incident. Then we'll sit tight."

On the helicopter, Karl, still dazed from injury and medication, smiled slightly as he touched Inge: "Sorry about our wrecked honeymoon. Will you take a rain-check?"

In similar condition, Inge smiled weakly: "I'm counting on it. And Fallingwater."

During the investigation of the incident that began the next day, the FBI joined the CIA and local authorities in examining the highway, the steep mountain slope, and the Volvo after it was retrieved by a special tow truck with a long cable.

The workers from the power company truck recalled meeting a dump truck many miles back, and the investigators concluded that such a truck could have caused the gashes in the driver's side of the Volvo.

"Still seems like a miracle they could have survived," said the reflective patrolman. "Those special seatbelts and the reinforced doors and roof made the difference between life and death."

After completing the analysis of the scene and the vehicle, the Federal agents cautioned all involved to refer any questions to them.

"Don't repeat this, but we suspect organized crime as the cause—and I don't think you will want them looking over your shoulder," said the leader of the investigation.

"We'll take it from here, but no doubt we will be back in touch with you—quietly."

With determination to match Mafia deviousness, the CIA and FBI proceeded steadily toward their objectives.

The surprise painting reproduction discovered by Karl and Inge in the book of art printed by Curtis proved to be the link to the Mafia. The investigation showed that a neo-Nazi working for Curtis Publishing heard of the Nelsons' discovery and sold the information to the Mafia.

Eventually, the FBI scored against the Mafia on several counts—attempted murder of Karl and Inge, threats against witnesses in that incident, racketeering involving stolen art, and laundering of money through publishing.

And the CIA finally completed an investigation that began with the OSS during World War II. It tracked down the actual painting and the ex-Nazi who sold the stolen painting to the Mafia—which then considered it too hot to exhibit or even donate, but safe to reproduce.

Karl and Inge also benefited from their own determination to recover from injuries. Each suffered a concussion and contusions. Karl hobbled during long healing from a broken left leg and arm, while Inge required plastic surgery to treat several gashes on her face and body—plus rebuilding her broken nose.

They thanked the many who prayed for and assisted in their recovery. With a touch of humor about the irony of the situation, they thanked the staff of Svensk-art for the handling the increased business that resulted from the publicity.

During lectures and radio and TV interviews, they expressed appreciation for the loyalty of the audiences for tolerating their limping movement and slurred speech during the recovery.

And they thanked the managers of the nearby American headquarters of Volvo—for the quality of the wrecked Volvo and for the replacement with the latest Volvo sedan.

Nearly recovered by the following Spring, Karl and Inge staged an international reunion, as their extended family and many friends converged on the Svensk-art compound to gather in an improvised arena and stay in a row of rented Winnebago motor-homes.

Now able to fly again, Karl and Inge put their Beechcraft Staggerwing through its paces as part of an air show for the reunion.

Naturally, the resulting publicity generated a major sales increase at the Svensk-art shop, at retail outlets and via mail orders.

So, at the conclusion of the reunion, Karl and Inge expressed their great pleasure for sharing past and present with family and friends.

"By the way," announced Karl, "because of the publicity you helped generate in this reunion, we've increased our sales so much that the additional income paid the entire cost of this wonderful party."

"So maybe you should all come back soon," added Inge, with a laugh shared by all.

In conclusion: LOS ANGELES AGAIN, THE YEAR 2009

At the Los Angeles TV studio, the roar grew in volume as Rex Lyon came back on stage.

"Great to hear that Lyon's Roar again!" exclaimed Rex. "I think you'll roar even louder when we start the second half of our show in the Lyon's Lair.

"Let me bring back our guest, Karl Nelson…and this time with the other half of the art-sleuthing team, his charming and beautiful wife, Inge Lindfelt Nelson."

The decibels of the Lyon's Roar rose to an even higher level than before, as the audience welcomed Inge and Karl.

"What a treat this is!" exclaimed Rex. "Two noted nonagenarians in the news, and both looking so calm and attractive. Both with doctor's degrees in art. Plus recent honorary degrees awarded in Wisconsin and Sweden.

"By the way, I love that slight Swedish sound in your speech, Inge.

"But how do the two of you sustain your pleasing appearance…at age 90?" asked Rex.

"Our Scandinavian heritage," said Karl, calmly.

"And cosmetics," added Inge, with a laugh echoed by the audience.

"Well, you might say we have a few of your cosmetics, so to speak, on display, Inge," said Rex. "We featured Karl's art portfolio in the first half of our show, and now we're pleased to display some of your paintings."

The audience cheered and clapped as the camera focused on a series of her paintings.

"Your paintings relate to Karl's, yet seem to be different and distinctive. How do you explain that, Inge?" asked Rex.

"For me, think plastics," she said.

"Like the famous advice in the movie *The Graduate*," laughed Rex.

"Oh yes, they're everywhere. See how pliable shapes flow through my art, like the lines of today's cars and appliances and furnishings…and even tools," explained Inge. "And my rainbow of colors reflect everyday life around us, too.

"But we've been involved together in life and art for 70 years, so I suppose we do tend to look alike and so do our paintings," smiled Inge. "Yet, in a strange contradiction, my paintings show the plastic form of Frank Lloyd Wright's Guggenheim Museum, while Wright's influence on Karl evokes the crisper geometric patterns of Taliesin North and Taliesin West."

"Okay Karl, how did the Wright influence on you come about?" asked Rex.

"Well, I did get lucky just before I started at the University of Wisconsin. I worked much of the summer as a volunteer at Taliesin near Madison. I even met Mr. Wright on my last day on my job there. And I've stayed in touch with others from Taliesin ever since, so they have continued as a profound influence on me and my art."

"Correct me if I'm wrong, but I recall that the two of you were heading for Wright's classic Fallingwater when a Mafia hit team used a truck to shove your car down a mountain and left you for dead," said Rex.

"That proved to be one of several miracles in our life," said Inge. "We've recovered almost fully," she added, with a sly smile, "though I could show you some of the scars I still have—but the censors might bleep your program."

"Did you ever visit Fallingwater...safely?" asked Rex.

"There...and many of the other Wright creations across the country," replied Inge. "Always inspiring...even though some were tainted with Wright controversy, too."

"How about an example of another miracle," urged Rex.

"Well, a bank of fog in Norway saved me when I was flying a Piper Cub, with a German Messerschmitt fighter plane in pursuit," said Karl.

"Not exactly an even match," interjected Rex.

"I banked a sharp left in the fog, but he didn't. And I survived, but he hit the side of a mountain!" exclaimed Karl.

"That reminds me...you two fly your own plane," said Rex. "Watch this clip we have of you climbing in your beautiful bi-plane and demonstrating some stunts."

"As you can tell," said Inge after the clip, "we were younger and braver then. Now we're just a couple of antiques... who admire that favorite antique...but on terra firma now."

"One last question," said Rex. "I gather you two have not only made enemies as well as friends from your involvement in art—but you've also made a pile of dough from art."

"Luck of the draw, so to speak," said Karl, as Rex groaned.

"We gained great knowledge through our investigations related to the art theft during the war, and that led to fees later for consulting and investigating for a wide range of clients," explained Karl. "And appearances such as this have added to our reputation and eventually to our bank account."

"Now we are subtracting instead," said Inge. "We've established art scholarships at several colleges and universities, we support the Jewish organizations seeking justice after World War II, we fund a variety of art workshops, and we underwrite books and magazines about art. So we hope that kind of investment pays off in more than money for a long time to come."

"A timely and meaningful end to our program today," announced Rex. "So how about another Lyon's Roar for these two amazing and wonderful nonagenarians!"

So Karl and Inge went out with a roar.

The End...of story...about Love and Art

www.ingramcontent.com/pod-product-compliance
Lightning Source LLC
Chambersburg PA
CBHW051448170526
45166CB00001B/160